testimonies of faith
from "out of the boat" lives

walking

on

water

Joey LeTourneau
& Family

Walking on Water

Written by Joey LeTourneau

Copyright © 2024

Bibliography

New Spirit Filled Life Bible. NKJV Edition (Thomas Nelson Bibles, 2002)

Bethel Church – Redding: 23, May 2023, "Faith doesn't deny a problem exists, it defies it." – Bill Johnson (YouTube)

Joey LeTourneau, The Life Giver (Shippensburg, PA: Destiny Image Publishers, 2012)

Joey LeTourneau, Revolutionary Freedom (Shippensburg, PA: Destiny Image Publishers, 2011)

Joey LeTourneau, The Power of Uncommon Unity: Becoming the Answer to Jesus' Final Prayer. (Shippensburg, PA: Destiny Image Publishers, 2013)

O'Connor, G. (2004). Miracle. Buena Vista Pictures.

Published by Seraph Creative in 2024

United States / United Kingdom / South Africa / Australia

www.seraphcreative.org

ISBN: 978-1-958997-97-0

eBook ISBN: 978-1-958997-98-7

To He Who calls us out on the water, and the many people who have walked there with us in various ways. Thank you!

index

index

Chapter 1- **Walking on Water?**

Chapter 2 - **Across Continents**

Chapter 3 - **Into Houses**

Chapter 4 - **Starting Young**

Chapter 5 - **As a Family**

Chapter 6 - **A Miracle Child**

Chapter 7 - **Alex's Story**

Chapter 8 - **Into New Seasons**

Chapter 9 - **On the Streets of Ethiopia**

Chapter 10 - **A Creative Miracle**

Chapter 11 - **Coming Back from Ethiopia**

Chapter 12 - **Learning Abundance**

Chapter 13 - **To California Again**

Chapter 14 - **To Israel**

Chapter 15 - **A Gold Country Treasure Hunt: Part 1**

Chapter 16 - **A Gold Country Treasure Hunt: Part 2**

Chapter 17 - **Growing Family**

Chapter 18 - **Running for Congress**

Chapter 19 - **Our 20 State Journey**

Chapter 20 - **Freedom U**

Chapter 21 - **A Strategic & Intense Time in the World**

Chapter 22 - **Birthing Abundance**

Chapter 23 - **Again**

introduction

introduction

"Now faith is the substance of things hoped for, the evidence of things not seen."
(Hebrews 11:1)

To walk by faith and not by sight can be challenging no matter how you spin it. It is a walk of grace as much as it is one of faith. There's a reason the Bible tells us that we live by grace, through faith. Both are essential. We can't supply the first for ourselves, but we do have control over the second part.

Some people are astonished at the life we've lived, especially with eight kids along the way. I mean, walking on water is enough just for one person, right? To step out of the boat and walk on water as a family of ten sounds like a whole other thing. But the truth is that this kind of living by faith as a family has made this path following the Lord, I dare not say, easier, but more possible. Why? Because everyone brings their own grace to the journey. Each of our kids carry something that we don't carry. And whether they are young or grown at the time, we couldn't have done this without them. And truly, they are also the first audience for this book. This book is us "picking up the memorial stones" after walking through the Jordan River and putting them all in one place for our family to remember and keep alive. And for others like yourself to hopefully be inspired by as well.

I wish we could share all the amazing miracles God has done. But truth be told, I don't think we could do most of them justice. From other moves not shared, houses, how rent was paid so many times, other bills, similar faith trips, and even just how groceries were bought many days; many of the Lord's timely, miraculous answers were/are so consistent day-to-day that they might sound redundant, even though that couldn't be further from the truth. But we have included many of the pillar stories from our families' journey out on the water.

It's important to say that our "living by faith" is far less about "our" faith, and more about Who one is looking at, Who we are listening to, Who we are obeying, and Who we are trusting. For me, at least, that's the remedial version of living by faith: keep your eyes on Jesus the entire time and then simply listen, obey and trust. Most if not every story in here starts by waiting on the Lord and hearing His voice. Then, it becomes about obeying Him. And the only way to obey Him in an unseen situation is to trust that if, and when you give Him room to show up and move, that He will. All the while, you feel the waves, the wind, and the pressures of the storm. Feeling them is one thing, but where we place our focus determines the truth we are living by in those moments. That's why Jesus wants us to keep our eyes on Him in those (and all) moments. Because then we are giving His truth greater reality than the truth of our circumstances. We are giving the truth of His presence with us preeminence over how the world and situations try to intimidate us. That's probably where the real battle is too. It's in our heads, those moments of decision, deciding between which one we will look at. And oh, do we feel the pressures and battles in those moments. That's where the worries, fears and "what ifs" from the enemy put their game face on. But that's also where we can lock our face upon His and learn not to live by what we have in our hands, but to live according to Who He is.

I would be remiss if I didn't make clear that it's not just about our listening either, but a lot of other people who have listened to God on our behalf over the years. Just like the number of miracles, we've lived from, there have been countless people who have been the substance of God's grace being sufficient, the substance of things hoped for while we wait for God to produce the evidence of things not yet seen. Different people in different ways in each different season. The goal is to keep our eyes and expectations off people and keep our eyes on Jesus as we step out of the boat and walk towards Him. We can't begin to name all the people or the ways that they, too, obeyed and trusted God's voice through every prayer, every gift or donation, and every bit of grace shown. But each one, known or unbeknownst to them, is a huge part of these "out of the boat" stories as well.

We want to say thank you to each of you!

Introduction

walking
on
water?

chapter 1
walking on water?

"And Peter answered Him and said, 'Lord, if it is You, command me to come to You on the water.' So He said, 'Come.' And when Peter had come down out of the boat, he walked on the water to go to Jesus.

But when he saw that the wind was boisterous, he was afraid; and beginning to sink he cried out, saying, 'Lord, save me!'

And immediately Jesus stretched out His hand and caught him, and said to him, 'O you of little faith, why did you doubt?'"

(Matthew 14: 28-31)

To "walk on water" may seem like a grandiose statement, but I assure you it isn't always a grandiose feeling. Like many miraculous or supernatural events throughout the Bible, we read of walking on water as a miracle meant to inspire our faith, which it can, but truly the reality of such is filled with so much more.

It may seem like a miracle that is distant from our lives when it is right there in front of us every day. What if walking on water was less a miraculous story or event, and more a consistent life path? What if walking on water was a daily invitation into the uncertain but certain call to follow Jesus on a very narrow, seemingly shaky path? What if walking on water was a picture of the reality of following Jesus through a tension of faith, viced between what we feel and Who we trust? What if walking on water was sometimes the only way to get into the place or promises that God has before us?

The process of a miracle is rarely what we think it is, it's just we usually get to look at it with 2000-year hindsight. Look at the feeding of the five thousand for example. It wasn't just something that Jesus did for them, it was something He called His disciples into with Him. When they bemoaned the circumstance before them, He told them, "You feed them." And He didn't mean go work harder and bring back more provision. He was essentially telling them, "You use your faith!"

And it's not like they took those five loaves and two fish, prayed over them and they suddenly went "poof," and became a miraculous pile of food ready to dish up for the crowd. No, this wasn't an event or miracle that felt all fun and amazing, at least not yet. Rather, the disciples were charged to keep putting their faith on the next plate. They had to keep giving, keep stepping forward out of their own apparent lack, through the pressure of seemingly not having enough while yet staring firmly at the fearful "what if" sign taunting them in their own minds. They didn't just feel the faith step once or twice, they had to put their faith on a plate 5000 times! That must have been excruciating.

Imagine their thankfulness each time another person was miraculously fed, only to realize they had to live it out again, and again. I can't say for sure, but I don't know if it likely ever "felt" like a miracle until after they were done, and everyone was fed. They were probably exhausted from pushing their faith over and again, hands on their knees, thankful they had survived only to look up and realize that not only was everyone fed, but they still had twelve baskets left over. The real miracle went beyond the five thousand who were fed. The real miracle was that the disciples accepted Jesus' invitation, took His charge, and kept stepping through the pressure of their circumstances.

Bill Johnson has an important quote about such faith: "Faith doesn't deny a problem exists; it defies it." That's what Jesus was calling His disciples to when He said, "you feed them." And that's what Jesus was inviting Peter into when He called him out of the boat and onto the water. He was calling him not just to step onto water, but to step beyond the limits of pressure or circumstance, and to live out a path and life that abandons certainty, defies uncertainty, and perseveres one step or one plate at a time. Living by faith, walking on water, whatever you want to call it; it's not necessarily the glorious miracle we make it out to be. It's the process of trust that teaches us to be in this world, but to live according to His.

I once ran into a Christian leader from a ministry we knew in a coffee shop and was both taken back and befuddled by the interaction. He had read one of our wild, testimony-filled updates and told me in somewhat of a joking, yet very real and pointed tone, "God told me to tell you to stop waiting until the last minute and making Him bail you out." I nodded and said thank you.

But almost all I could think of as I smiled and walked away was, "that doesn't sound like the God I follow, or read about." With God, it's not about being bailed out, it's about partnering with Him in something that is beyond us, beyond our ways.

The truth is, our personal path then, and now, of walking by faith and trusting God to "bail us out" of so many wild missions and adventures throughout our lives has never been about surviving a tough situation or circumstance. It's been about God telling us, and teaching us to not just "have" our faith but to consistently use it.

Whether it was trusting God to show up on a Tuesday night amid a transition season when we didn't know how we'd pay a bill or get groceries, or impossible, adventurous moves overseas, it has been a string of testimonies of continuous, deep learning of how to join God's in His ways, instead of staying comfortable or stuck in our own. Living by faith hasn't been about getting by, but about taking ground. It's rarely been comfortable. And often, we have found ourselves wondering, "haven't we passed this test yet," haha. As if faith is just a test or a miracle. Rather, it's been a sequence of hopeful obedience turned into persevering surrender, to praise-filled testimonies to doing it all again. You feel every ounce of it. You hope you are finished with that test. And then you learn that He didn't call you out of the boat to walk ten feet to Him, but to teach you to walk that way for the rest of your life. That's walking on water.

Our desire for this book is that it would strengthen God's existing invitation in your own life and family. These stories aren't just for us, rather, they are prophetic testimonies that speak to how He has invited us all to live with Him. Granted, it will look very different for us each. But as circumstances in the world or your lives change, or perhaps look and feel more like stormy waters out on an uncertain sea. Remember, Jesus isn't calling you just to survive the storm, He's teaching you how to walk through it. The faith that you use in those moments, defying the feelings of the storm, is what God will use brick by brick, seed by seed, to establish His kingdom. It's in you, and He's drawing it out of you for His greater purposes.

across
continents

chapter 2
across continents

Destiny, our firstborn daughter, Mercy, and I took a trip many years ago that changed our lives forever. It started by seeking more of the Lord and what He wanted to do, or was doing among the nations, and it continued and finished with us being carried by grace through more of an answer than we were ready to receive.

I was working with Youth for Christ International at the time to coordinate their global youth prayer movement. As we looked at that role, mixed with the calling and mission God had been putting before us for years we realized that we needed to base somewhere other than the United States. We knew we were called to give life to the broken and empower the powerless so that they could give life to others. But before any of this could happen, we needed an impossible answer from God to make it through a vision trip so we could get to the mission we were called to.

The trip was going to cover seven African nations in seven weeks. We would fly into Rwanda in February and leave for home from South Africa in April. We had five other nations in between, including island nations; with trainings we were scheduled to conduct and a lot of people to meet and learn from. The trip was a way of asking God where He wanted us to set up our base. And we needed an answer only He could give.

Even though the trip was scheduled, we had very little of the funding for the trip. However, even a couple weeks from our departure date, we still felt a strong peace from the Lord that we were to go, regardless of what our funding or circumstances looked like. I asked the Lord about our need, and simply heard, "It's done. Just as the Jordan was not parted until they stepped into the river, you must go, and you will walk through the river on dry ground." So, that's what we did. We could not fulfill our calling to give life, without God pouring out a miraculous path.

We had enough funds to purchase our ticket to Rwanda in February and purchased our return from South Africa in April. But we had nothing firmly booked in between them. We were told by all our contacts in the various nations what we needed for food, lodging, transportation, etc., and it totaled about three thousand dollars. We had five hundred dollars for a family of three and all seven nations. But God!

Our travel agent tried to hold onto as many "possible flights" he had set up for when provision came through, but the spaces would be taken up quickly. We boarded our first flight and were on our way to Rwanda.

Our time in Rwanda was one of the longest of all the nations we visited, and according to their words, they "exploited" us. Wow, did we feel it. But it was well worth it. We met so many amazing people, incredible relationships, and saw God bring forth lots of fruit. Our trip was at its end, and we still did not have funding for our next flight to Ethiopia. The day before we were scheduled to leave Rwanda, we checked into how much the flight to Ethiopia would cost purchasing it locally. It was fourteen hundred dollars for the three of us. We continued in prayer and kept walking forward towards God's purpose for us. By late that afternoon we received word that fourteen hundred dollars exactly had just come into our account, and they wired it immediately from the office in the States. Praise God! We even ended up on the same flight we would have left on had we been able to take the original flight our travel agent had scheduled. Also, it was the only flight available destined for Ethiopia that week. Otherwise, we would have missed our next meetings and been delayed by a week. So, not only did we receive provision for the flight, but we also received more faith.

While on the flight to Ethiopia I began to inquire of the Lord how we were to get to our third stop, Kenya, at the end of our time in Ethiopia. Apparently, I had received more faith but wasn't full enough yet, since I was already worried about the next one. But God's grace and faithfulness are bigger than me and the Holy Spirit gave me strategy. I felt led to seek out our primary contact in Ethiopia upon arrival and ask if she knew of a Christian travel agent. So, on our way from the airport to the hotel late that night I asked. Surprisingly, she had a good friend who was a believer and a travel agent and assured us she would take us to see him later in the week.

Before leaving Rwanda, we had checked with the airline what it would cost to go from Ethiopia to Kenya, so we would be prepared. We were told all three tickets would cost $1100.

The time in Ethiopia was going very well, and we immediately sensed a connection in our spirit, one that started even as our plane touched the ground. As we deplaned, Destiny heard in her spirit, "I will turn your hearts towards these people."

During our first few days in Ethiopia, no new provision had come in towards our trip. But the morning we were scheduled to meet with the Christian travel agent, we found out that six hundred dollars had just been deposited into our personal account. Just over half of what we were told the tickets would cost. But we were thankful to receive any provision at that point. We arrived at the travel agency, they brought us some incredible espresso macchiatos, and started to check our flights. When they asked for our passports to book the tickets, I had to inquire how much this was going to cost. "Six hundred dollars," they answered very casually. We handed them our personal debit card attached to the account that six hundred dollars had just been deposited and suddenly, had our tickets for our next stop, Kenya.

As we mentioned before, we had five hundred dollars cash to cover all our food, lodging and expenses. In Rwanda, costs were at a minimum because we were blessed to stay with a local missionary family. In Ethiopia, we had about three hundred dollars worth of expenses, leaving us with two hundred dollars for the next five nations.

Knowing this, our contact in Ethiopia told us the one thing we would want to do is avoid staying at one specific guest house in Kenya, which would cost us five hundred dollars alone for the length of our stay. So, upon arriving in Kenya one of our first questions was to ask where we would be staying. We laughed, and maybe cringed a little on the inside, when they told us the exact same place we were just warned not to stay. But our Kenyan contact told us it was the best place for us to be and that we would have one month to pay our bill, which gave us a timeframe extending through the first week of April. Praise God, He gave us a better place to stay and provided through the grace of time.

Our time in Kenya had more travel than ministry, viewing different aspects of the local ministry and the country. But on the final day, the day before we were to travel far south to Botswana, we were supposed to lead a training with their volunteer team of young leaders.

Most of the trainings we led were patterned from Acts 4, teaching the individuals how to come together, inquire of the Lord, seek God's vision and strategy, be filled up and be prepared for Him to send them into His purposes for their lives and ministry. This requires some teaching time, but a lot of practical prayers and waiting time, teaching them how to go into God's presence to listen and be empowered. Destiny and I were very moved during this time watching how moved by the Spirit this team was. They were one of the most united groups we met with, and thus, when they came together to wait on the Lord in prayer, they experienced even more than others.

We were moved during the prayer time, but we were overwhelmed and humbled as it concluded. Just as we were wrapping up an incredible time in God's presence, the local director, who knew of some of the miracles God was pouring out during our travels, stood up and began sharing some of the testimonies of our trip with the group of volunteers.

Before she could even finish her last words, one young volunteer stood up, walked to the kitchen and grabbed a bowl. "They have been walking by faith, and living what they teach. So we are going to do the same. We are not leaving here until this family has enough money for their flight tomorrow to Botswana." (The need was $1600) Our eyes got even bigger, our jaws dropped, and tears were pouring down our faces. In fact, I can hardly think back on this time without weeping. This young leader lowered this bowl near his pockets and just started emptying. He passed the bowl around and everyone did the same. These were volunteers of a local Youth for Christ mission in Kenya. They had no salary, very little for themselves already, and now they took everything and began to pour it out on us. We were broken over this outpouring of selfless, abundant love.

The leader then took the bowl of money into a nearby national ministry office they were connected to and began to tell them the testimony of how God had just moved and these young leaders' act of faith. Before we knew it, they were so moved by the extravagant, free giving of these young volunteers that the office decided they would believe God for the difference until it was provided otherwise. The next day, we got on our flight to Botswana overwhelmed by how God, once again, had poured out not just what we needed, but allowed us to receive much more from the nature of His love.

Once we arrived in Botswana, we knew that we had to buy the rest of our trip in one chunk, flights and stops that would take us through Mauritius, a small island out east in the Indian ocean, Madagascar, and finally, South Africa. This chunk would cost us four thousand dollars from start to finish with the flights. But we knew God had not allowed us to miss any of our schedules, and we had not even been late for one meeting despite relying on God to take us across the African continent one miracle at a time.

We had less access to communication where we were in Botswana, and I was very sick. Our account showed no funding available, but we had to keep moving forward by faith so that we could receive what God promised to give.

Two days before we were to leave Botswana for the island region of Africa, we got an e-mail that the exact amount needed for our tickets, four thousand dollars, had just come into our account. We were elated, and just praising God! This chunk would get us through each of our last stops in Mauritius and Madagascar and back to South Africa in time for our mid-April return home. We called our office in the States to contact our travel agent immediately. Unfortunately, all the space we were holding for that four-thousand-dollar total was now gone and we were back to square one. The only flights available would now require an extra flight to make one of our connections and the total was almost six thousand dollars. She said she would look around some more, we said we would continue to pray and believe, and I told her I'd look forward to hearing good news soon.

We went directly to our knees, and thanked God for all He had done already. We had been walking through this river on dry ground, and we had not even missed or been late for a meeting. In fact, we reminded the Lord of this, claiming His faithfulness and promise that we would walk through the river on dry ground. We held it all back up into His hands and left it there before we went to sleep.

I woke up to a phone call the next morning from our office in the states. "Joey, it's a miracle! You'll never believe what happened! We got the space for the tickets, now you arrive early, we even added an extra connection that will help smooth out the trip and the tickets will cost less than four thousand dollars. Praise God!"

After Botswana, we had a very busy but wonderful trip in tropical Mauritius. Someone referred to it as the Hawaii of the Indian Ocean, and wow, were they right! It was a fantastic week taking people into God's presence to see them empowered further and if that wasn't enough, the island itself was breathtaking. It was one of those extra special blessings in the trip where God lavishes even more on top of the abundance you're already receiving. We were staying in someone's home right on the beach in Mauritius. They welcomed us into their family with open arms and blessed us beyond measure. We left for our flight to Madagascar that first week of April but had become very aware of the date the night before we left as our guesthouse bill in Kenya for five hundred dollars was now due.

We were still living from the initial five-hundred-dollar expense money we had started with. How it had made it this far was already water to wine, but we did not have enough to pay the bill. I woke up that morning of our flight looking up, knowing the Lord still had more to pour out. As we went out the door, we found an envelope on the table from the family we were staying with. Inside the envelope was exactly five hundred dollars. This was starting to get crazy! But we serve a Crazy-Abundant, Life-Giving God who has crazy amounts of love to pour out on us. We just need to step into a position to freely receive the same grace He has called us to give freely to others.

After this miracle, we had an amazing time with the team in Madagascar. What a wonderful place, and incredible people. We had several days of awesome sessions, and growing relationships with people we still love and miss today. God did a few other miracles during this time in the islands before we landed for just a couple of days in South Africa to wrap up our trip, meet with some leaders and board a plane back home.

But just before we left the airport, I could not help but grab a piece of the testimony we had just walked in with the Lord. God gave us far more than a vision trip across Africa. So, as we walked out to the van, I scooped up three rocks, one for Destiny, one for our daughter Mercy, and one for myself, because those rocks, like the memorial stones they picked up after crossing the Jordan, were proof of the testimony that God had indeed led us across the river on dry ground. All the while, we had rent, utilities and other bills back in Denver to keep up on. God is good! He provided for all step-by-step.

This seven-nation trip testimony is a small picture of what much of the rest of our lives has been since that time. Not all the stories are in one trip such as this, but the same process of listening to God's voice, of stepping out onto uncertain waters, and of watching God make an unlikely and timely path forward are all vital parts of how we've lived the last almost twenty years. And, how He continues to challenge us to live today.

into

houses

chapter 3
into houses

Did you know you can walk on water into houses and lands?

I have been blessed by the family heritage I have inherited. There is one testimony that has always been foundational and has given life to many in and through my family.

My mom grew up with three siblings, and they were rather poor. Her dad had been very ill with a heart condition and was in and out of the hospital at least half of every year. Through this health crisis, they reached a time when their businesses all went bankrupt, and they could not pay their bills. They were renting a house, had little food available, and my grandma was working six days a week just to survive. She was exhausted, and her husband, was in the last year or so of his life. The crisis only seemed to increase when the owner of the house they were renting approached and told them they had to be out immediately, they were converting the property into a bank.

My Grandma was exhausted. She did not have enough time, energy or resources to do all that was necessary for her family. Her husband was slowly dying, and she surely didn't have enough money for another house.

One day, her only day off that week, she began to drive the neighborhood with my mom, who was about nine at the time, and her younger sister, then two. As soon as she began in this hope, she was already exhausted. The overwhelming need and task she was called to walk through felt like too much. But my grandma had never been much of a feeler, she was a believer. They had just begun their search when my grandma, done in, pulled off to the side of the road, declaring, "Let's pray!" "Lord," she cried out, "You know we do not have the money for a house, and I do not have the time to look for one. But you know we need a house. So, Lord, we ask that you please give us a house."

After that simple prayer of faith, they turned around and went on with the laundry list of other needs to survive. The next day, a neighbor from across the street came and knocked on their door. "I am being transferred," he said. "You need a house, and I don't need this one anymore." He lived across the street in an enormous house which spanned three lots. "I would like to give you my house. You don't need to give me a thing, as I understand your current situation. Maybe sometime in the future, we can work something very small out for payment, but I do not want you to worry about it."

My Grandma, my grandpa, my mom, and my aunts and uncle were desperate, but they knew that they served a God of "more." Even their prayers did not have to be extravagant, but simple, because they knew a God who was and is extravagant in His love and giving towards us. The next day, the whole family and their friends literally formed an assembly line across the street. From the house they had to leave, to the one they had just been given freely, they passed item after item, from family member, to friend, to family member, to friend across the street and through the door until the house was full. They asked for more, but they got more than they could even ask for.

We need to be people who live in more. That more isn't about the item or need at hand, but about the faith we've been called to walk in. We spend much of our lives pursuing more of the wrong things but need to learn to channel that same vigorous hunger to the right kind of "more." My family was desperate when they cried out to God. We can learn something from this, but not just for those times when we are desperate. What if we applied the miracles we hear and speak about from desperate situations to our lives and calling before we become desperate. Sure, these desperate situations will still find us now and then, and we can seek God in the same way then, just as my family did. But what if we became pro-active with our desperation? What if we sought the more that is available to us, before the need arises? Instead of only asking for more when we need it, let us live desperate for more so we can give more to everyone all the time! But first, we must learn to ask, when we are desperate, and even before we are desperate.

My grandfather, who I never got to know, passed away about a year later, but they saw God begin to give life into the family, the extended family, and many friends and acquaintances through receiving that house. Freely they received the life that house brought to them, and freely, for years, the family, that house and the family atmosphere within it gave more life than it ever received.

The apostles in Acts 4 experienced the exact same kind of receiving. Freely, they received more than they could ask for, because they asked for the right kind of more.

They cried out with prayer in this way, then they began to receive as freely as they asked. They received one of the most powerful answers in Scripture because they received something that started a multiplication that could not be stopped.

"And when they had prayed, the place where they were assembled together was shaken; and they were all filled with the Holy Spirit, and they spoke the word of God with boldness." (Acts 4:31)

Their current surroundings were "shaken." Something rocked their world. God answered them and gave to them in such a way that when they received what He had to give, even the place they were staying would not be left the same. Something beyond human answers came into that room. Why is it that we expect so little of God? What would happen if we asked, and received like the apostles in Acts 4? God always wants to exceed our meager expectations and lead us forward into greater promises that can multiply to many others. We must learn to ask according to the more He is capable of, according to who He is. But it is not worth asking unless we have such expectation of Him that we will step and also position ourselves to receive what only God can do.

ethiopia house

We were approaching our moving day. Destiny, my wife, was pregnant, our only daughter at the time, Mercy, had just turned five, and we were on our way to live in Ethiopia. The only problem was, we didn't have anywhere to live in Ethiopia. Our local contact was working very hard to find what she deemed was the right house for us and we were trusting her to do so. Finally, she found one. She was sure of it, so we agreed. However, we agreed with the understanding that first, we would have to secure the funds.

Most house rentals at this time in Addis Ababa required at least six months but most often one year paid up front. We told our contact in no uncertain terms that we did not have the money yet. The owners of the home were asking for one year up front of over twelve hundred dollars a month. This was far too much for us. We preferred a modest home and had always lived in apartments up until this point. However, our contact assured us that this was where we should be location wise and asked us to trust her. So, we did. It was a large home (which turned out to be a good thing with how many people we ended up housing), but it was a very old home, and pretty worn on the edges as well. The kind of place most usually call a "fixer upper" to say the least. Except, unfortunately, I've never been much of a "fixer.'

Anyway, with the fees we would have to pay for the transfer, organizational fees, taxes, etc. we needed $16,000 before we moved. Of which we had none. Though we didn't have the money, we soon found out that the home had been accepted on our behalf without us having any idea. We wouldn't have wanted to be irresponsible and commit to that which we couldn't afford, but such liberty was taken for us. We had no choice but to trust God and keep stepping. However, we didn't find out about such an agreement until two days before the deadline to pay. We were under the impression that if the money didn't come in, we'd simply lose the house. You can imagine our feelings when we learned that we were under a guarantee to pay $16,000 in two days, or else still be held liable for the contract and lose the house to another renter at the same time.

All that day, we prayed. We believed. We had seen God move in miraculous ways many times before, but still found ourselves in this anxious place between very real pressure and our purpose in Ethiopia. The next morning, I woke up to an e-mail at 6 am. It said the full amount had to be transferred and on its way by the end of the day. Though our account remained at zero, and without a prospect in sight. I stilled my heart sitting on the laptop of our dining room table, boxes packed up all around me, family living with us at the time and felt that still small assurance in my heart. My reply was brief but closed with this. "We look forward to writing you with a good report very shortly."

Destiny, Mercy, my mom, my sister, Jackie and a close family-friend, Jeff, were all part of agreeing in prayer and praise that morning (as well as many prayer partners!). I shared the e-mail, but they already knew the intensity of the pressure and circumstance. We decided to praise. We looked back at 2 Chronicles 20, a life passage for our family, and remembered the impossible battle won by praise. So, we sat in a small circle on the floor, now a few minutes after seven and did not plead or beg — we simply praised! We began to thank God for His undying, unending faithfulness. We praised Him for allowing us to trust Him through such fire. We thanked Him in advance for the answer He already knew. Then, we just got up and went on with the day, praises still ringing through our hearts. Praise changes our perspective and silences pressure while highlighting the power of trust.

We hopped in the car to take Mercy to pre-school when I got a phone call. It was from our office back in Colorado. "Joey, guess what?" A co-worker from our office exclaimed. "You just received an anonymous gift that was sent in for $16,000." I lit up with a smile, nearly doused in tears, and thanked God and my friend once again. We set up the parameters for transfer, and I called Destiny and the family back home to let them know of what God had done. Then, just hours after writing to our contact in Ethiopia of the good report we believed we would be sharing soon, this time I called her instead. We didn't care about the roaming or international charges. She had to be brought into such a God-given miracle. We watched His purposes become possible, and His promises come alive!

There are many worldly realities, cultural pressures and intimidating lies of the enemy that are used to make us fear stepping forward. Most of us want badly to live a life of significance and purpose, most of which is already anxiously waiting inside us, probably afraid that we aren't going to let it out. Thankfully, the Bible gives us a lot of testimonies of weak, imperfect, fearful vessels who have multiplied through much lack and walked straight through many barriers. It is these testimonies, with God's intimate presence as our Source, that have led our family to surrender ourselves to the Potter in a way that has allowed Him to leave many of these same fingerprint testimonies all over our lives. We have been broke, empty and totally dependent on God to meet us, with no backup plan or any ace up our sleeves. These have not been extravagant crusades of faith or courageous runs into battle, but from simply listening to God, obeying His voice and living His word, we have been left to trust Him instead of ourselves or any supposed security we're told we should have. He has always been more than enough. Sometimes, He is just waiting for us to depend on Him enough, to be weak enough for the world to see how truly good and faithful He is.

the how

What I didn't tell you yet about that story is the unique walk of faith, of obeying a peculiar directive from the Lord, led to that testimony becoming reality.

As I said we were in California preparing for our move to Ethiopia. We were scheduled to go back to Colorado for some important organizational meetings with leaders from around the world in attendance, and I was supposed to be there.

We were planning to drive as a family, as we did most things, and leave just in time to arrive in Denver for the meetings. However, just a couple of days before we were supposed to leave, I felt the Lord speaking to my heart, "It's not time yet, don't go." Slightly taken aback and surprised by what I sensed God saying, I naturally went to my reasoning first. "But Lord, I'm supposed to be there for these meetings. They asked me to be there, and I committed that I would. What am I even supposed to tell them as to why?"

I wrestled in prayer a bit, trying to make sure it really was the Holy Spirit's conviction, and not self, that I was feeling regarding this word. I came away from the prayer time even more convinced. So, then, as I did with anything I felt from the Lord I went to Destiny to confer with her and see what she was hearing/felt and make sure it lined up. She agreed and felt a peace about the directive, so now, I just needed to make the phone call and somehow explain why we couldn't come.

I decided it was best just to be extremely transparent and clear when I called to talk to the leaders of our organization. To paraphrase, "Hi, I know I'm supposed to be there for the meetings this week, and I would love to be part of them. But for some reason, as I pray, I feel like the Lord is saying to wait, and not to come yet. I don't know why, only that He will make it clear when we're supposed to come, even if we miss the meetings."

They graciously agreed and valued following God's lead on the situation. After all, they had seen God show up in some crazy and special ways already through our seven nation Africa trip. And they knew we needed to follow the Lord's voice, and not man's conventional ways as we prepared to move our family and ministry base to Ethiopia. I was incredibly thankful for their response.

But now, we had to wait—and keep listening. We had to hear "when" God wanted us to go. For approximately two weeks, we waited, each day inquiring of the Lord, yet still not feeling a release to start our trip to Colorado.

Finally, about two weeks after the meetings the Lord spoke loudly in my spirit; "Now, go. It's time." Gathering myself, we had very little funding now to make the road trip. Even our vehicle was suddenly not up for such a long trip so we would need provision for a rental van on top of everything else. We started to pack by faith and get ready to go. When those moments come, it's important not to follow our circumstances of what they say we can or can't do, but to step forward onto the choppy water where it looks like we might even sink. God said it was time to go, and that is what we had to align with.

As we packed and prepared to leave the next day, some funding came in late that day for a rental van. We hustled to the rental company and just hours before we were supposed to depart, we had our van for the trip. I'll always remember being in the garage with it that night, late, packing up all that we had prepared before we had the van. And enough provision had come in to make the trip with food and gas as well.

We arrived in Colorado, still not knowing what the purpose of the delay was for, or why it was this time we needed to be there. We went through a series of meetings with those in the organization, and with other prayer partners and supporters. The President of the organization had become a mentor to me, and though he was busy with close friends who were in town from their native Australia, we were able to have a nice lunch at their house and share more of what God had been doing, and how He was setting things up going forward.

By the end of the trip, nothing unusual had happened. There were no miraculous moments that made it clear why we had to wait those extra two weeks, why we missed the international leadership meetings, or why God said to come during this specific time. However, we knew that we had obeyed God's voice and that was the only part that we could control. The rest was up to Him.

At this time, it was later in February, and we were arriving back to our temporary home in California, to prepare to move to the home God and our

Ethiopian contact had set up for us in Addis Ababa. We came to that time in the testimony that began this house story, when God provided at the last minute the $16,000 for our house, a house that eventually became even more of a miracle house for all God did in it, and through it. But some weeks went by after that miracle came through and we learned a little more about where that "anonymous" gift had come from at that most opportune moment. It came from the friends of the President of our organization, the ones from Australia who happened only to be in Colorado that week God told us to go. It came from an uneventful but wonderful lunch on a random day that week, a lunch that was full of little more than sharing testimonies such as these. If we hadn't listened and obeyed in the small, seemingly insignificant things, we wouldn't have been aligned with the testimony God wanted to bring about, or the home in Ethiopia He wanted to give us and use for so much.

3 - Into Houses

starting young

chapter 4

starting young

I grew up in a family whose life was missions and faith. And this set the foundation for me to start my own faith journeys very young. Though I had the examples in front of me, it still wasn't something that was just taught to me. Rather, it was something I was empowered in by learning to hear God's voice. That is what has begun every faith step in my and my family's journey. It's never about this courageous run into battle, or an attempt to do something crazy or miraculous. In fact, sometimes, just like it was for those like Gideon, it can look or feel more like reluctant obedience.

To me, that reluctant obedience is actually a good thing, because it helps you know you're not doing something just out of self, or out of your own will. It is part of partnering with God in obedience no matter what things look like and learning to trust the results to Him.

One of my early faith steps was when I was eighteen to nineteen years old. I had been a part of organizing and speaking at several city-wide events spanning the Denver metro area, but I wasn't trying to plan another one. I was simply doing what I had learned to do those past few years, getting on my face before the Lord, worshipping, entering His presence and waiting on Him to show up and or speak. I would often lay there silently for hours but for one outward prayer, "Lord, please teach me the things that I don't even know how to ask for."

I wanted to learn His ways, not just an amped-up version of my own. I figured God had perspective that was beyond my ability to even ask for, and that's the kind I was desperate for. I simply wanted more of Him, and to learn His perspective and ways more than my own.

That led to one specific time waiting on the Lord when something new was birthed. We talked often of testimonies and the power they hold, as they are literally God's fingerprints on someone's life or a situation. They help reveal

God's invisible realities as He makes the otherwise impossible come to life. And, as I mentioned, I had been involved in planning city-wide, and specifically student-led events. But that experience didn't make me want to plan another typical event. If anything, even back then, I wanted something different. I wanted something that wasn't about a program, that wasn't about a sermon or message, just anything that lifted Jesus up and tugged on the premise of John 12:32, "When He is lifted up, He will draw all people unto Himself."

But this specific prayer time, I felt the Lord begin to speak, and lead. Little by little God fed me breadcrumb after breadcrumb. I felt like He spoke to put on a gathering called, "Our Day at Calvary." That it was to be held on Memorial Day, the day we remember those who have died for us. And that the event was to be held in the center of downtown Denver, right in front of the State Capitol building, in Civic Center Park. One of the strongest things I sensed from the Lord was not to make it about preaching or music, but simply a full day of worship and testimonies.

I felt the gathering wasn't supposed to be put on by any one specific church, denomination or organization, but that it was supposed to be a coming together of hungry one's from many churches, denominations and organizations. Back then, this wasn't common, for multiple reasons. First, you needed the financial support of one group or the other, and two, there was of course, a lot of division among different denominational beliefs. But our goal was to make Jesus' prayer for a John 17 kind of unity come alive even in the planning of the gathering, let alone for the people who would attend.

One last major specific I felt from the Lord was that as we would be looking to hold the event in the center of Denver and in front of the Capitol, that I was supposed to get the blessing of Governor Bill Owens to do so. As an eighteen-year-old in the suburbs, I obviously had no such connection or access to the governor. But I knew that if God was calling for it, then it was important, and He would make a way.

I started by calling a few trusted friends and intercessors whose hearts would resonate with what the Lord was giving me, and to begin by having prayer meetings together about how to move forward. These meetings were little about agenda and planning, most of that I would share at the beginning to get the logistics out of the way, and then it was time for the main part of each meeting, and that was to get on our faces together and let the Lord speak and lead us about how to move forward.

As we begun to take steps forward, two practical logistics were at the forefront: 1. How to reserve the amphitheater/park in front of the Capitol, and 2. How to start to get a letter into the hands of Governor Owens to ask for his blessing.

When I eventually went downtown to inquire about the city park, we found that the Memorial Day date was available, praise God! But they gave us a large laundry list of things we had to have at the event to comply with their ordinances. We had to have so many porta-potties, food vendors, and other things of that sort. And, considering we didn't have any funding except what God organically provided, we were going to need a lot to see this come together.

So, we just continued to take one step after another. By faith, we filed the paperwork for the park, and I started to ask around to the handful of people I was sharing with, inquiring whether anyone had a connection to the Governor. On my third call, an intercessor friend of ours said she was friends with a State Senator, and if I wrote a letter, she would see if he would be willing to pass it on. Thus, that's where I began. I prayed, wrote the letter, and entrusted the envelope into her hands, not knowing where it would go from there.

Meanwhile, we started praying and putting together a list of various people we might ask to share a testimony throughout the day of the gathering, as well as a list of those who could come and lead worship. We didn't have the funds to pay any big bands to come, but I did have a growing connection with the lead singer of a very popular Christian worship group at that time. After a few discussions, and much prayer, this worship group said they would be willing to come for a small fraction of their normal concert fees because they believe in the focus of the gathering. We didn't have close even to that amount yet to pay them, but it felt like God had provided for the bulk of such already, so by faith, we said yes and decided we would trust God to provide for the rest at the appropriate time.

All the while, I met with and started to share with a variety of community and church leaders not just about the event, but the story of how God started speaking to me about it, what was to be involved, why, as well as all that was starting to bring together; people started to become so encouraged and excited they began connecting me all over the state. Leaders, students, prayer groups from all different churches, organizations and denominations started to get involved. Each one brought what they had in their hands. It might have been a little bit of support, a connection to someone else, the use of a massive $20,000 sound system, a testimony, or a willingness to pray and contend for what God wanted to do that day. We had nothing in our hands to make this now large gathering come together, but as various people throughout different parts of the Body of Christ started to come together, we watched God provide for need after need. We all stood in awe watching what God, not man or any organization, was putting together.

It wasn't long before I received a letter from the State Capitol, more specifically from the Office of the Governor. I ripped open the letter and found not only encouraging words from Governor Owens, but he had written a blessing for what God wanted to do that day in front of the Capitol and in the center of downtown.

All the little things like vendors, porta-potties, etc. started to get lined up. The program of worship and testimonies was coming together, and we now had an army of people praying and waiting on the Lord with us. It was a nine-month planning process that was organically ordered by the Lord. And our planning meetings remained focused on the same. We would start out by putting the necessary logistics on the table, lay out the needs, and then spend most of our time thanking God in worship and waiting on Him in prayer for His direction.

A few days before the gathering, we were starting our last meeting and still had thousands of dollars needed for everything to finish coming together as scheduled. While we probably wanted to do the human thing and worry and talk about our needs and how to address them, we did what we had always done; we thanked God and waited on Him for His answers in prayer. About halfway through the meeting, someone came and tapped me on the shoulder as I lay there on my face, they motioned for me to come over to speak with them quietly so as not to interrupt all that was going on in God's presence.

"Joey, we just received an envelope with a check. It's enough to cover the last remaining needs."

I went back to where we were gathered around the Lord and shared the incredible news with everyone. The already praise-filled room erupted into even more, all together watching God do what only God could do.

The gathering itself was amazing, and though it was a very hot day, the high-end sound system we donated rang loudly throughout the entire city of downtown Denver with worship and testimonies. We watched the homeless of the area drawn one by one to what was happening in front of the Capitol, and I'll never forget seeing them laid prostrate on their faces worshipping in the presence of the Lord. Truly, God was lifted up that day, and He drew men unto Himself. As much as we all loved the fruit of that gathering, and the thousands in attendance from multiple states, many churches and organizations, the part that rocked us the most was the nine-month faith process of watching God lead us and build this gathering one step at a time from scratch. We didn't plan from a budget, or with a big name on the platform, rather, the whole process was led by the voice of the Lord and us coming together to follow Him and see His will established.

aka
family

chapter 5
as a family

Around that same time at eighteen years old, through many of my early faith endeavors, God started to open doors for me to speak at events and conferences around the country as part of a movement called Revival Generation, made up of a few of us "student leaders" from the Denver area.

Destiny and I weren't married, so obviously, I didn't have a family yet. However, I'll never forget one moment that I'll always look back on as somewhat of a prophetic knowing with the Lord. I was flying home from a different state, on the terminal transport train in Denver International Airport. Suddenly, while holding the rail inside that train car, I had this feeling and prayer inside me that said, "I don't want to be doing this when I have a family. I don't want to be doing itinerant ministry without them, always away and separate. I want to follow You, Lord, together, and live out our mission and calling together as a family." I had no idea how important that moment would be and set the table for so much.

As you read before regarding our seven-nation trip across Africa, our firstborn daughter, Mercy, was very much a part of that faith journey. Though many would say she was just four years old at the time, God helped us to include her all along the way. We talked with her and taught her even then about not just praying but also being quiet and listening to God with us. I'll never forget one such moment on the couch in our living room.

I said, "Okay, we're going to practice listening to God. I just want you to be quiet for a few moments, and simply say, 'Jesus, do you love me?'" And then listen in your heart for what He says.

So, we closed our eyes and were still and quiet together. After a very brief time, I asked her, "Well, what did God say?"

"He said 'yes,' that He loves me," she replied.

"That's wonderful," I answered.

Then, following up, I said, "Ok, now we're going to be still and quiet for just a little bit longer. I want you simply to ask the Lord, 'What do you want to say to me?'"

So, we did. She did.

"Well," I started to ask. "What did God say to you this time?"

She answered, at four years old remember; "He said that I have a Spirit inside me that helps me to be good.'"

I was floored.

As much as we talked to her about God. Prayed with her. Taught her how to listen to His voice and the importance of the Bible. We hadn't really talked yet about the Person of the Holy Spirit in specific terms. So, for her to get this directly from the Lord was something special. And she was right!

Mercy was a big part of the seven-nation trip. Especially in Rwanda. It was there that she gave her life to Jesus, and the next day, joined me with a translator to share her testimony and lead almost two hundred more kids to know and believe in Jesus as their Savior. As we left the school grounds that day, Mercy sat in the back of the rugged SUV while kids chased the vehicle. Unbeknownst to us, she rolled down her window, opened her backpack and started handing out her books and coloring books and anything else she could find to one child after another. The other leaders there in Rwanda joyfully named her "Mercy the Missionary," and she has had a heart for people around the world and has been in the middle of missions ever since.

Destiny was four months pregnant with our second-born daughter, Galilee, when we first moved to Ethiopia in 2008. Since we didn't have a car, Destiny,

Mercy and I walked the streets of Addis Ababa almost every day through some very rough parts of the city. People gawked at us as foreigners in those areas, blonde-haired and blue-eyed, but even more for the growing baby in Destiny's belly as we walked the streets.

Galilee was born later that year in Addis Ababa, Ethiopia and grew up with a growing Ethiopian family all around her. Our house was full each day with people we were employing by faith or who we were mentoring and discipling. Her life started as a step of faith to still go through with our move while Des was pregnant, and to have Galilee born in another country. And ever since then, Galilee has been right in the middle of our faith adventures, eager to start forging her own.

Before we moved to Ethiopia, one of the things Destiny and I had in common long before we ever met was a love for Africa and a desire to do missions there. It's one of the things that lit up between us as we grew in our relationship. We also had discussed a heart for adoption but didn't know when or how God might bring that about.

Before our move to Addis Ababa, on that seven-nation faith trip across the continent, we also visited a very special orphanage connected to a church and some new friends of ours there in Addis. I'll never forget that moment we were conducting interviews with the kids. We were asked about each of their story and what God was teaching them. When we visited with Aynalem, one of the older girls in the home, I felt like I heard this whisper over my shoulder; "She is your daughter."

It wasn't "she will be your daughter," rather, "she is your daughter."

Little did I know God was already building Destiny's connection with her as well, putting the same thing on her heart. And isn't that just the Father's way? Romans 4:17 says that God, "calls things which do not exist as though they did." We see people as unsaved, lost or broken, but God already sees them as sons or daughters. And that's how He was speaking to us regarding Aynalem, who was nine years old at the time.

See, we had no earthly way to start an adoption process, let alone match up to its cost or laundry list of requirements. We were only around twenty-seven years old at the time, didn't have any guaranteed income to qualify, didn't have a home, were moving to Ethiopia, and to adopt Ayni, we would be disrupting birth order and separating her sibling set. Absolutely nothing matched up in the natural. But God! He told us she was already a part of our family.

So, even though we didn't know how it was going to happen, or when, we kept moving forward with the belief that she would soon be our daughter, and we started talking to the local leaders about how it could become possible.

Once we moved to Ethiopia, we started visiting that special orphanage home weekly. We spent time playing with the kids, eating with them, and spent a lot of time praying with them and teaching them to wait on God and hear His voice. God moved so powerfully in that group, and we'll share more about that later, but we were starting to really build a bond with all eights kids who lived in the home. Besides Aynalem, now, there was a couple of new girls there, sisters, and our spirit really connected with the older sister, Kelemua. Her passion for the Lord stood out, and she gave hugs that reminded me of my wife's hugs—like someone is wrapping a fierce, intentional love of the Lord around you.

Kelemua was just a little older than Ayni, but God was building a family bond for us with her too. Again, circumstance made it sound impossible by all that we had been told, especially with some unique parts of Kelemua's situation. However, God spoke loudly to us and confirmed it was right to press forward and persevere by faith, to trust Him to move every mountain and to make a way for her and Ayni to both be our daughters.

Now, we were believing God for two older girls to be our daughters, despite not owning a home, nor having a guaranteed income, having any savings, and despite all the issues with age and family dynamics as typically seen by the State within International adoptions, at least back then.

We were told by local Ethiopian leaders we could try a local adoption, which would be much cheaper and with far less hoops to jump through or mountains to overcome. But, they said we would have to stay in the country with them for two years before they would legally become our daughters, and we would risk the possibility that the governing bodies could change the rules (something that happens often) and end up putting the girls in a difficult situation. We prayed and felt the Lord said to trust Him through the bigger, more unlikely path of the international adoption. That's when we had to go back to the U.S. to start compiling any paperwork that we could to start the process.

Back in the States, our friends the Dutton's graciously let us use their suburban to travel all around the U.S. for the first half of our trip. And after a very full, faith-adventure filled time back in the States, we arrived back in Ethiopia with our adoption process started and we saw God begin to move many of those mountains that were in the way of our girls becoming our girls. However, there were still a few big unanswered questions and a very large amount of adoption costs we were trusting God to provide for.

However, there was one specific situation on our trip back to the States that had our attention. There was one boy at the home, Nebeyu, who we were very close to and felt a strong connection with. He was the oldest and still didn't have a family yet. We prayed about adopting Nebeyu as well, but as we prayed God made it very clear that we were not to adopt him, but to trust God and pray forward the family that He had for him.

For our trip back to the U.S., we had made a somewhat of an album of pictures of many of the kids from the orphanage, and of kids from the streets we were working with. We had daily and weekly prayer times with many of these kids, asked them questions, and were often amazed at how God started to speak to them, and through them for that matter. We wrote down much of what they shared from those prayer times and included some of those quotes with their pictures in the album. We took this album with us all throughout the U.S. as we traveled, and it encouraged so many people. We, of course, had a couple of pages in the book dedicated to Nebeyu, his story and what God was doing in his life. And, as we prepared our adoption paperwork for Ayni & Kelemua, we spent a good bit of our trip praying for God to raise up and bring forward Nebeyu's family. This was so at the forefront of our hearts that one night Destiny had a dream of sharing a hug with Nebeyu's adoptive mom. When she woke up and told me about the dream, you could tell it was more than an ordinary or passive dream, but she was still shaken from the reality of the encounter—and the hug in that dream!

Towards the end of the trip, we went to visit a family who graciously lent us their truck for the rest of our time back in California. We had met the father of the family, Rick, when he visited Ethiopia and stayed with us some months prior. Now, we were getting to meet the rest of the wonderful Cross family! His wife, Wendi, opened the door and welcomed us warmly, with hugs and amazing hospitality. We weren't in the door for even a few minutes when Destiny pulled me aside quickly to say, "Joey, that was the hug! That was the hug from the dream with Nebeyu's mom!"

You could tell she was rocked by the moment! Though, of course, we didn't say anything, no matter how much we wanted to. But we did have a wonderful evening with them. And Destiny and I couldn't help but smile with wide eyes every time we saw them go through that album of the kids, because they kept stopping on Nebeyu's page—and left it open on his page much of the night! However, nothing was talked about and as we finished our time in California, we didn't hear any more about the possibility of them adopting. We had to leave it with the Lord and keep on praying.

The last couple of days before returning to Ethiopia, we were staying with my aunt and uncle. We wanted Nebeyu's family for him so badly, we fasted that week for a breakthrough to come. I remember praying in the shower one morning, asking the Lord, "Are you going to do this? Are you going to raise up a family for Nebeyu?"

I heard a quick, still small voice of a response back from the Lord that surprised me as I felt Him say, "If you let your heart be made keen to another."

"What?" I thought. "What does that even mean?"

"But yes, Lord, yes! You know you have our yes! Please just show us what that means."

And that's where we left it as we headed back to Addis Ababa.

Almost immediately upon arriving to our home in Ethiopia, we had an appointment with an American social worker for a home study. That year, with our daughter Galilee being born and our two adopted daughters "hopefully" coming into the family soon, we were suddenly going to go from a family of three to a family of six. Before our social worker wrapped up our home study that day, she paused, and shared about another difficult situation. She said that she had just been made aware of one orphaned infant in their transition home. The baby was six weeks old but was almost two months premature and was transitioning towards another missionary family who was adopting him. However, this social worker had just been made aware of how intense this baby's special needs were. The needs were so severe that the nurses at the transition home could no longer take care of him. And with his special needs, the agency didn't feel like the adoption could go on as planned, so this little special-needs infant needed an emergency home and caretaking. The social worker, there to make sure we were fit to take in Ayni & Kelemua, was now asking if we would also be willing to foster this little boy who apparently too much for those already giving him care.

We were a little wide-eyed to tell you the truth. Not because we didn't want to help this precious little guy, but we were already growing our household by so much, taking a big leap of faith that still needed several more mountains moved, and we had even less medical training (NONE!) than the nurses who were already caring for him. And she wanted us to take him? Our hearts always want to say yes to such, but as crazy as our life sounds, we still want to be responsible for our growing family's sake.

At the same time, we remembered that unique word the Lord spoke to me in the shower that morning before we left the U.S. while we fasted and prayed for Nebeyu's forever family: "If you let your heart be made keen to another." Is this the "other" Lord that you were prompting us about? We weren't sure yet, so we asked the social worker if we could have a couple of days to pray and get confirmation. She said yes, but that the gravity of the situation really needed an answer in the next 48 hours.

As was common in the area, the power was out that day and evening and thus, the internet was out as well. We had plenty of time and quiet to press into the Lord and wait for His confirmation.

Morning came, the power was restored, and I jumped online to catch up on e-mail from what I might've missed the day before. And there it was. It was an e-mail from the Cross family that had come in the day before during the exact hour the social worker had asked us if we would take this little baby boy with special needs. They were adopting Nebeyu!! We were so thankful, and almost couldn't believe it. And realized quite clearly that we had our confirmation. Since it was while praying for Nebeyu's family, asking if God was going to bring them forward that He asked us if we would let our heart be made keen to another, it was only perfectly fitting that we found out about such an answer in the very moment that "another" was put before our faith, and our yes.

We called the social worker immediately and let her know that we would take the baby boy. The rest of his story was a process and a miracle that we'll share more about in the next chapter. But before we close this one regarding this part of our family story, we must tell you how God continued to work in these adoption stories.

See, in the process of fostering the little baby boy, Sidamo, God used that to bring about extra grace and provision that ended up covering almost our entire adoption for Kelemua and Ayni to come into their own special places in our family. That was a miracle in itself.

But then there's Nebeyu, who has very much had his own incredible story with the Cross family. But I can't not mention where that story has led. Remember, we wanted Neb to be part of our family. We wanted to adopt him. God said no. He had a different family. He raised that family. He provided for Kelemua and Ayni to come into ours. And then Kelemua and Neb started talking more. God started moving in each of their hearts. Soon, they got engaged. And now, Neb really is part of our family after all as our son-in-law.

God's full-circle miracle of family is the best!

5 - As a Family

child

chapter 6
a miracle child

This is the story of Sidamo, Samuel, and Micah. Three stories about one child of God. (As originally shared in my book, The Life Giver. Pgs. 169-177, Destiny Image, 2012)

sidamo:

Within a day, this little boy, Sidamo, arrived at our home. Our hearts broke to see how small and how sick he was. He appeared to be just on the edge of life, a delicate flower starved of water, light, or roots to grow from. He was so fragile we worried about his ability to make it through the night. Here in the States, he would have been in ICU, likely with tubes to feed him and help him breathe. In Ethiopia, love and grace were his only chance; love and grace were our only chance as well. God's grace was all we had. But, His grace, no matter how difficult the situation, is always sufficient. Welcome, Sidamo!

samuel:

When Sidamo arrived with our family, all we could do was call on the grace of God. None of the circumstances of our natural lives lined up with his arrival, but God's desire was evident, we were to simply love him.

Love is all we had. This precious little boy could barely sleep. His stomach really wrestled against himself, causing him to hunger deeply because he could not retain food, so much so that he would cry for food at the same time he cried for it to be taken away. His body was brittle and could barely move his limbs. From the moment he arrived, he would have terrifying panic attacks, sometimes one every other minute. They weren't seizures nor were they just fits of discomfort, rather, Sidamo appeared terrified during these attacks, as if he was being tormented by the devil himself. We had never witnessed anything to this extent before, let alone with an infant.

We had no medical background or experience. But we had love. And every day, as the difficulties grew in those first four months with Sidamo, it felt like through this little baby, Jesus was asking us the same challenging questions that he asked Peter over and again In John 21, 'Do you love me?" Every day, we pleaded for the Lord to revive, strengthen and deepen our love. Our love was not enough. We needed His love to care for this special little boy.

We used what we had in our hands, and even more, what we had in our hearts. But as we found out time and time again, even what we had in our hearts was not enough. Sidamo needed more. Sidamo needed love that could not come from man alone, he needed the love that comes from the redemptive, life-giving nature of God. Sidamo needed grace, new love, and so did we.

The first thing we did was write out promise cards, written on with two scriptures a piece and placed these under all the mattresses he would sleep on. This way, he could rest on the promises of God. We believed the name he came with, Sidamo, was part of a grief that God was redeeming him from, so we prayed for a new name. With God, we gave him the name Samuel for this season in his life. In the Bible, Samuel was such a child of promise and destiny. We had to speak this same kind of promise and destiny over this broken little boy and believe for God's vision for his life.

We carried him around each day, all day, snuggling him close to our body, worshipping and praising God over him, and speaking God's word over every area of his life. Since Destiny was nursing our youngest biological daughter, Galilee, at the time, she even tried to give Samuel the same. We did not have the medical equipment to keep him alive, but God is much bigger than that. For the first four months, each day seemed to get harder and harder. Almost every week we had to seek God for new wisdom and revelation as to how to care for this baby boy, Samuel. Each day, we had to dig deeper and rise higher for a new kind of love, one that was far beyond our human nature to give, and for a love that would give life to someone battling to survive.

Our flesh showed itself too often, and as much as Samuel needed grace to survive what was inflicted upon him, we needed grace to survive our own flesh. Each day, we had to receive from God that which we did not already have.

God gave us several breakthroughs, giving us words of wisdom from praying of friends and family, revelation from His Spirit, and strength to give more love and grace to Samuel. God brought us an incredible Nanny to help during the days, another believer to help pray and praise over his life. Eventually, this Nanny became a very special part of our leadership team in Ethiopia.

And she, too had her love challenged through this fearfully and wonderfully made little boy.

We received Samuel when he was about six weeks old, after being born approximately two months premature. We noticed early on that along with the tormenting panic attacks, Samuel could not make eye contact and lived in what we can only describe as a fog that seemed to consume him.

One night, I had just finished feeding him and was heading back to bed praying for him when the Lord suddenly gave me a vision. It was a simple picture, but a dreaded one. It came amidst my prayers for Samuel and seemed to be in regard to him as well. The picture was of a person, cloaked in dreary, lifeless oppression. It was not a picture of death but was the epitome of the lack of life. There was nothing horrific about the look of the person in the picture, but the temperature and perception of the vision made me think of the thief and stealing life.

I happened to Skype with my mom the next morning. I began to tell her of the vision and found her in disbelief. That same day, before I called, she had just been reading something further on deliverance, cases beginning with similar trauma as Samuel had in the infant stage. She couldn't believe the vision I described because it was so like some of the testimonies she had just read.

That day, our whole family fasted for Samuel and inquired of the Lord to gain insight into how to pray. God gave us about eight promises or bullet points to specifically pray, declare over him, and trust God for His deliverance and freedom. Aynalem and Mercy sat on the floor with Destiny and I as we gathered around this precious but hurting boy. We laid hands on him and had a very simple prayer time, taking the authority of Christ and simply declaring the verses and words God had given us over Samuel. Immediately, we saw something break open. And within twenty minutes, Samuel began to make eye contact with us for the first time. The fog that once plagued him began to dissipate and we soon noticed that his tormenting panic attacks began to slow down incredibly.

Two days later, Selam, who was working as Samuel's nanny, came over to the house for her time with him. We did not tell her anything of what God had done. But within thirty minutes of being with Samuel, she came running into the room, "What happened to him? He is so much different. What happened?" We laughed together with joy and thankfulness, simply sharing how God had set him free.

We had a few more instances such as these where God brought us tremendous breakthrough, a word of wisdom, or a strategy of love. And we needed every one of them. Our love never felt like enough, and that was the truth. We needed more, not just for Samuel, but for every other person we would encounter for the rest of our lives.

We later found out how much Samuel was up against while in our care after he was adopted by our cousins. Even when he arrived in the U.S. with his new family, six months after we received him, he was immediately declared as "failure to thrive." Before leaving us, he still could not eat and what he did eat usually all came up. He vomited an average of about thirty times per day. He was immediately diagnosed with cerebral palsy, and tests actually showed that his brain was literally split in a very unusual way. He's had a number of surgeries on his stomach to keep food down, he was given a feeding tube and was even placed on valium at all times so that he could bear what his insides were going through. Finally, on top of everything else they found out amidst all this that Samuel was legally blind.

This precious little boy, Samuel, was a fighter. He had no medical care for six months while dealing with these conditions as a premature infant in our home in Ethiopia. He lived off the lifeline of God's grace. We all did.

Samuel is a part of our lives we would never change. Many times, we felt like absolute failures and the worst of sinners, unable to do enough for him. Jesus simply wanted to ask us the same question he asked Peter so that we would be prepared as Peter was prepared. "Do you love Me?" I think of Samuel and I hear that question. I think of Samuel and can't even begin to share about how difficult a season that was. I think of Samuel and I think of someone who changed our lives far more than we changed his.

micah:

Micah, this is Samuel's new name and is part of the redemptive grace God poured out on Samuel when He brought breakthrough. God moved the mountain in Samuel's life and brought Micah into a new, lavishly loving family that was the perfect fit for his life of promise. The family that adopted him are our cousins. They have fought and battled, and praise God, they have seen incredible advances. Micah has been an answer in their lives just as they have been such an answer in his. It is a beautiful picture of the Spirit of Adoption and how God is moving among His children, and in His family.

"For you did not receive the spirit of bondage again to fear, but you received the Spirit of adoption by whom we cry out, 'Abba, Father.'" (Romans 8:15)

Sidamo and Samuel both shook and cried out in pain in terrifying panic attacks. But Micah has been drawn into God's family, where now he cries out, "Abba, Father," according to the redemption and love God has used to give him life, and life more abundantly. Micah was, and is, a miracle.

alex's
story

chapter 7
alex's story

I first met Alex on a vision trip to Ethiopia before our family moved to live there. Our primary contact in the country was driving us around, answering all our questions while giving us a taste of the culture. She kept telling us about this one young man she'd known since he was little, Alex. He had been away from the capital city of Addis Ababa for some time now, ever since he got out of prison. He was in his early twenties and a couple of years before, had been falsely accused of taking the wrap for something a group of his friends had done—though he had put himself in the wrong place with the wrong people.

She wished we could meet him, and so did we. So much of our hope in Ethiopia was to mentor at-risk youth and raise up local young leaders to be those who brought change to their communities and nation. When I started to hear about Alex, my spirit leaped. If only I could have the chance to connect with him, but last he had been heard from by our contact he was hours away down country and not easy to get a hold of.

Then, we were on one of our drives through the city amidst hundreds of the usual passersby over the medians and around the streets when our contact stopped suddenly, rolled down her window and burst out with a yell, "Alex!"

He had just come back into the city that week we happened to be there. And here was our chance encounter on the streets in the middle of this huge, international city. I had only a brief interaction with him at first, but it laid the groundwork and I could see what was within him, knowing he was different and believing he had more to offer than he knew.

See, Alex had grown up on the streets alone, living in a plastic house since he was seven years old. His dad died when he was two and five years later, when his mom re-married, her new husband (as was customary at the time) expected her to relinquish her kids and start anew with him. His story rocked us to our core and made our hearts well up with tears. Thankfully, it was only the beginning, and we were about to get to play a big part in his redemption story, and he in ours.

I knew with all of me that Alex was our link to the streets, as Ethiopia—Addis Ababa in particular—was home to an inordinate amount of street kids and orphans. But first, we wanted Alex to see himself in a new way—through value, through love, through purpose, and belief.

We started discipling Alex each day, and even had him move into our home as part of our family. It was only about one week into this process that God challenged us again. We were very much living by faith, not knowing when or where our next provision was coming from—and we only had $250 cash left to our name (more than many other times) as we began to set up our lives and homes in Ethiopia. God spoke clearly to our hearts and asked us to give it all away, to Alex.

Now, this presented multiple challenges. First, we didn't know what we would live off for the next period of time or how God would provide. Second, Alex was still pretty fresh off his life on the streets, and we didn't want a sudden large chunk of money to send him in the wrong direction when we saw God doing so much in his life. That was a lot of money for his context. But we felt strongly from the Lord that this was of Him, for us and for Alex. Our job wasn't to reason our decision with human wisdom, our job was to obey the Lord and trust Him to show up where Alex and us needed it most. So, later that night we went and grabbed all the cash we had left. We asked Alex to join us and said God had something He wanted him to have. We then took our handfuls of the local currency and placed it in his hands. This could have been like winning the lottery for him compared to what he had grown up with. But Alex didn't jump for joy or run out of the house with a sudden list of items to buy. Instead, Alex just stood there and trembled before the Lord. He was overwhelmed by the gift, and by what was being entrusted to him by God, and by us.

It didn't break him in a bad way, it broke him in a God way. The next day Alex went and did three things with the money. First, he bought groceries for our family for us all to live off for that week. Second, he bought himself a pair of good shoes for walking the streets as he often did, and as we had begun to prayerfully do together each day. Third, he went to the bank and had them break up a majority of the cash into small bills of the local currency, that way, he could walk and pray with the Lord as we had been teaching him and he decided he would give it away little by little when the right opportunities arose to love people and seize the plentiful harvest that was all across those streets of Ethiopia. Each of those bills became like seeds, more than money, they were faith, hope and love that he was depositing everywhere he went.

Before we knew it, we started to see a huge harvest of multiplication grow across the streets; God was redeeming and empowering lives. But it all started by empowering Alex. We had to let go of what we had in our hands, and we had to trust Alex to the Lord as well. We couldn't just teach him, we had to give him the opportunity—even the opportunity to fail. And that opportunity multiplied much further than anything we could have done or built on our own.

Now, Alex has started multiple businesses, and empowered far more street kids and emerging, young leaders through those businesses. He has helped countless kids from the street who grew up like him, and helped many moms that were in a similar situation to his mom. Already, he has helped almost fifty moms from the streets start new businesses, and discipled them, to help give their families a new foundation. And his own mom and step-dad, who abandoned him to the streets when he was seven, have come back into the picture. Both were sick and struggling, Alex forgave them both for what they had done to him, and helped care for his step-dad while he was sick and dying. Since then, Alex has taken care of his mom, through multiple illnesses and many needs, the very mom he could have been most bitter towards. He has started his own family, his daughter is his pride and joy and Alex is such an amazing Dad!

Found on the streets, discipled on the streets, Alex became a "father" to the streets and took all that was done to him and flipped it upside down, not only being redeemed but redeeming others. He doesn't have a big salary or house, because everything he receives, he keeps giving away. But he has planted more seeds than can be imagined by simply using what he has in his hands, trusting God to supply the next day for Himself, and for the next one on the streets he will soon meet.

7 - Alex's Story

into new
seasons

chapter 8

into new seasons

We were just finishing our second year in Ethiopia. It had been a unique and hard season with Sidamo/Samuel, but very rewarding and fruitful as well. That year was less about being on the streets, and more about seeing so much of what was planted the year before start to sprout.

Every day our house was full! Guests and groups from the streets, from the U.S., from orphanages, churches, etc. all spent days and nights with us in our home. We were preparing to go back to the U.S., for a couple of months for meetings and to renew our Ethiopian business visas. Before we went back, I felt the Lord highlight a book I had written ten years before, _Revolutionary Freedom._

After originally writing the rough draft and doing a little more work on it, I felt the Lord tell me to "put it on the shelf," and that it was for a later time. Every now and then in the years to follow I would pick it back up, edit a little, add a bit here and there, and then put it back on the shelf. But as we were closing this second season in Ethiopia, I felt the Lord saying to start to get it ready to publish. I didn't know when that would be, but He highlighted a large, well-established publisher that we had read many books from. Even though they accepted at best 1 out of every 100 submissions, I felt confident from the Lord that this was to be our publisher and that the book was key to get ready for the next seasons to come.

We went ahead with our trip back to the States, traveled quite a bit, our adopted daughters Ayni and Kelemua (though we changed her name to Anna) got to experience the U.S. for the first time and meet much of our family and many friends. We sent off our passports to the Ethiopian Embassy in Washington D.C. to have our visas renewed and we were eagerly preparing to return to Ethiopia.

Thankfully, enough provision had come in to buy our return tickets to Addis

Ababa, but we were still waiting for our passports and visas to come back to our family's home in California. Time continued to pass, and our return flight was coming quickly, but our passports with visas had not arrived yet. We had gotten word they were approved, but then when we went to track them, they had virtually disappeared from the system.

I called the main office of the United States Post Office and at first, they, too, were having difficulty tracking them down. After a thorough search they got back to us and said, "We're sorry, we don't know what has happened. It is as if they dropped off the face of the earth." As you can imagine, that's not exactly what you want to hear from the highest post office when it involves our whole families' passports and visas, with our flight leaving for our home in Ethiopia within a couple of days.

I called our travel agent, and we pushed back our tickets another week. It looked like we were going to need to get whole new passports, and fast! Then, we would need to re-send those passports back to the Ethiopian Embassy in Washington, DC, to get new visas once again. All in all, this was going to cost us $2,000 to have redone, and we barely had $100 to our name.

We were praying and waiting on the Lord for His provision, but nothing was coming in. It was anguishing, extending our trip to the States, living on air mattresses in our aunt and uncle's living room, barely getting by each day while having such expectancy for what the next season held back in Ethiopia and all God had been doing there.

We kept calling our travel agent and pushing back our trip a few days at a time while we waited. We were getting further into summer and adoption travel was starting to fill up all the space on the route of our flights. We pushed our tickets back one more week to the next Friday, but he said after that there wasn't any more room for the next month or more because adoption travel was really starting to boom in Ethiopia at that time.

We prayed those next couple of days, and on Sunday, I found myself crying out to the Lord. I was confused. This felt wrong. I was trying to figure out if this was just warfare from the enemy trying to block us going back, or if there was something else that was in our hands that we needed to do something about.

As I went to prayer to ask, suddenly, I felt a light bulb go off in my spirit!

The book! God had told me before this trip that it was almost time to publish the book. Was I supposed to do something with that now before we left the States? It felt right, like God was waiting on us to put that piece in motion. So, I spent the rest of Sunday looking at the application and requirements from the publisher God had highlighted months before. Finally, late that night I had gotten it all put together and hit "send" on my submission. I climbed into bed and felt this supernatural wave just wash over me. It was like a rainforest of the Spirit, total peace, dripping and refreshing all around me as we had just unloaded whatever burden we were carrying.

The next morning I was up early as usual, and our daughter Mercy came out to me. She was just seven years old at the time.

"Dad, I had a dream last night. We had money come in the mail and we got our passports!" She exclaimed, as she and the other kids had been praying with us for God's answers.

"We'll see," I said. "But that's wonderful. Let's see what God does!"

Just a couple of hours later I received a call. A check for $2,000 had only now arrived. I called to thank the donor who had felt prompted to send the funds and his response was unusual.

"You know," he answered. "I tried to send the check weeks ago for $1,000, but it was returned to me for some reason. Then I sent it again for $1,500, and I don't know why but it came back again! So, I finally wrote the check for $2,000 and tried one more time. I'm thankful it finally made it."

Ahh, we had to laugh at that one. God knew the amount we needed, and He knew that we were supposed to release the submission of the book before we went back and got caught up in the immense movement we were seeing with the street kids across Addis Ababa. It wasn't exactly a comfortable situation, but a timely one.

Immediately, I called the passport office a few hours away in San Francisco to get an appointment for the next day, Tuesday, for emergency expediting of our new passports. See, our last flight option was Friday, and we needed the passports in time to still send them to the embassy in Washington D.C., have our visas processed, and get them returned to us by Thursday if we were going to make our flight. It sounded like an impossible situation, but seeing what God had done in the last twenty-four hours certainly spiked our faith!

We got the appointment and left early the next morning for San Francisco. We waited through the looooonnngg lines at the Passport agency when finally, it was our turn. They said usually they can get them back to us within a couple of hours, but their computers were having issues and with the line of requests, they couldn't make any promises. We prayed and trusted God knew what we needed.

At about 3 pm we got a call that our passports were ready, praise Jesus!! We called the embassy in D.C., and reminded them of our situation and that we would overnight the passports immediately, including an overnight envelope for the way back to get them by no later than Thursday. As a family, stroller and all, we ran a few blocks to FedEx and got the envelopes sent off just in time before the overnight, next-day cutoff. We were exhausted, emotionally and physically. It was out of our hands now and all we could do was trust God to bring them back.

We spent all of Wednesday preparing by faith to travel back on Friday, eagerly waiting and hoping to see our passports (with visas!) arrive in time. Sure enough, later Thursday morning, I got a call from our aunt and uncle at the address our envelope was coming to, and they told us they had just arrived, and we could come pick them up! We were beyond relieved, ready for this whole ordeal to be over and to get back to our home, and all God was doing in Ethiopia.

However, a funny thing happened. Right after I picked up our new passports and visas from my aunt and uncle's house, not even half an hour later, someone else from their family called us.

"Hey Joey, I think your passports arrived. You can come pick them up whenever you're ready."

"Huh," I wondered aloud. "We just came and got our passports a few minutes ago. What do you mean we can come pick them up?"

"I don't know, but they're here."

I turned around and drove back to their house and sure enough, they were right. Except, it obviously wasn't the FedEx envelope we held in our hands. It was an unmarked, plastic bag with our original, old passports and visas inside with a simple note: "Sorry for the inconvenience."

We didn't even know what to say after that. But God had moved mountains, got us both sets of passports in time and we were on our way back to Ethiopia. It was only a couple of weeks later that I received an e-mail from that larger publisher, you know, the one that only took 1 in 100 submissions. They wanted the book and were ready to start the publishing process! Thank You, Lord, the whole ordeal was worth it. Once again, the sometimes exhausting but always worth it "process of a miracle," or two or three miracles. Thanks God!

on the streets of ethiopia

chapter 9
on the streets of ethiopia

One of the foundation points of our mission and family in Ethiopia was walking the streets according to John 10:10. "The thief does not come except to steal, and to kill, and to destroy. I have come that they may have life, and that they may have it more abundantly."

The whole base of the movement now multiplying outward in Ethiopia began with us learning to live an offensive mentality on the streets, wherever we went, whomever we were with. We did not have a vehicle during our time in Ethiopia, so we were very reliant on public transportation, and spent a good bit of our time walking across the city. As much as this could be an inconvenience, it was a blessing in disguise. It kept us with the people. Walking the streets helped build relationships, it taught us the culture in a very raw form. As we mentioned previously, Destiny was pregnant with our second biological daughter, Galilee when we first moved there. This was quite a sight. Destiny, Mercy and I walking the streets, blonde-haired and blue-eyed, a pregnant belly protruding from Destiny, endlessly walking and trying to love and give life as Jesus would. You could say we stood out just a little bit.

This was not always easy, but it was always worth it. This drew a lot of attention at times, which sometimes could be used as a platform to show Christ's love, and other times it drew very unwanted attention full of threats, criticism and the like. As we woke up to approach the streets each day, we had a choice; offense or defense? The enemy would try to attack our thoughts. He would try to frighten us from feeling safe to freely walk, give, or freely distribute life through love. The enemy used his fear tactics to try and bully through our thoughts, he did not want us to play offense. And on those days, we had to really battle not to be swayed back to a fearful, defensive mentality.

I remember one day in particular that was quite the battle, but quite a victory. I woke up that morning with a clear mandate from the Lord. Go out on the streets with Alex, and just walk. God had something He wanted to do. However, we had no money. We had seven birr, which at the time was the equivalent of fifty cents, to support the ten people currently living in the house. Our power was out that day due to the power ration that frequently takes place and our propane tank for our stove was empty. The enemy was trying to set us up, but I felt God wanted me to go.

We needed funds not only for the family, but for a number of the street kids we were taking care of. God reminded us not to look at the circumstances, but to go out and give life according to what was in His heart rather than what was in our hands. I was just about to leave when Destiny suddenly felt very sick. I had not seen her in such pain for a long time. My first thought was whether I should stay home. Nope, couldn't fall into the temptation to play defense, God told me to go out and play offense. So, I went to Destiny and laid hands on her while praying. She agreed with me in faith, looking only to the Lord, and quickly felt better. Praise God!

I was just about to walk out the door when a quick need popped up. Our toilets were not flushing due to some of the issues with water and plumbing so we were flushing our toilets with buckets. This is a very common thing. My family needed me to fill the bucket before leaving because it was too heavy for them to lift on their own. I went to fill the bucket and while leaning over my back suddenly went out. I could not remember the last time my back went out. It felt like a crack had just spread up and down my spine. It was some of the worst pain I could remember in a long time. Again, the enemy was trying to keep us from offense. I couldn't remember a morning with this much warfare.

As I laid on a special ball we have for stretching, now with Destiny praying over me, I inquired of the Lord as to what I was supposed to do. The Spirit spoke to my heart, "When you walk out that gate, your back will be completely healed." Well, that was that as far as I could see. It was time to go.

Just before leaving, I grabbed my ATM card. Our account was empty, but I felt prompted by the Lord to take it with me just in case something might come through. Alex and I approached our gate, sought the Lord as usual to ask Him to lead us, and then stepped out to walk with the Lord and give life to those who were hurting, broken or begging on the streets.

About a block after leaving our house I realized that all my back pain was now gone. By the grace of God, I had left it at the gate. Alex and I couldn't get a bus after waiting at our stop, so we continued on foot. Sometimes that was best anyway, it provided more opportunities to pray over people and ask God how to join Him.

We had a couple of errands to run in the process, so we headed towards the direction they were in. Just to walk the streets and smile His light towards someone was opportunity enough on most days. But sometimes God had something more. This day we were close to where our stops were and were passing a row of shoe shiners, a trade that is very common among the streets and even more common among kids who live on the streets.

We walked past a long row of shoe shiners and the Lord caught my attention. There was a light over this young man, but due to our own fleshly agenda, we kept walking. The Spirit was nudging me to get my shoes shined. I didn't want my shoes shined. I was wearing trail shoes that really did not need to be shined. But the Lord would not give up. Maybe it wasn't my shoes that needed shining, perhaps it was me, and, or this man. The Spirit was convicting my heart over and again to go back and meet him. Finally, I obliged. I told Alex that there was someone back behind us God wanted us to meet, and I needed to get my shoes shined.

As he began to shine my shoes, we began to talk. Much of our conversation was through Alex's interpretation. The shoe shiner's name was Abraham. He came to the city from down country looking for work. He came from a Christian background but was away from family and support. Just as he finished shining my shoes, I asked if we could pray over him. He nodded, so we laid our hands upon him and began to bless him. We blessed him to be who God had called him to be, to arise and shine. It was a time to give life simply by reminding him of the Lord's love for him and calling forth God's purposes within him. It was a very simple time, but clearly, God ordained it.

As I stood up to leave, just after saying goodbye, I sensed the Lord speaking to my heart again. This time, the directive was quite different. God was directing me to the ATM. I reasoned that there were zero dollars in our account and the ATM does not spit out money if there is zero money in there. However, I knew this was from God. We reached the ATM building and I walked up according to the word of the Lord. Then I asked the Lord how much I should take out. "The maximum amount," which was 4000 birr, or about $250 at the time. I put in my card, entered my pin and, voila! 4000 birr came right out without any hesitation or question. I was a little stunned. The money was not in the account. This ATM had never allowed money to come out that was not in there, I even knew its usual message by heart. But this day, that message did not appear. Jehovah Jireh appeared!

We now had the full provision we needed to take care of the street kids that night. Praise God! We also had enough money to get food for home and our family as well as purchase a new propane tank. Thanks again, God!

The enemy clearly did not want us to go on offense that day. But every time we put our hearts back on offense, and giving life, God showed up. Living from a mentality of defense can sneak up on us. As I said before, we had to battle it in a variety of ways many days while walking the streets of Addis Ababa. Each time, we had a choice to make, offense or defense? Survive life, or give life? We did not always choose correctly, but every time we did, we saw God show up.

In one of my previous books, The Life Giver, I shared about my grandmother, my mom's mom, and the stories of how she freely received and so freely gave, even out of the very little they had. But I am also blessed by such a heritage from my dad's side of the family and the testimony of my distant uncle, R.G. LeTourneau. He is most often known as a forerunner and inventor in the earth moving equipment industry and used his success to make quite an impact in ministry and missions as well. LeTourneau University in Texas was founded by him and his work and passion in many areas. In fact, he has often been referred to as "God's businessman." But, what we must know from his life, a testimony I personally look to glean from, is that one of the greatest reasons for his immense success and impact was the fact that he knew the kingdom dynamic of generosity. R.G. freely lived into this kingdom economy that we can often be so hesitant to embrace. R.G. got to a point in life where, unafraid of what he might lose, he gave 90% of his income into the kingdom, believing in what, or who, God might gain.

"Don't forget how big God is and how good he wants to be to us if we will only let Him."
- *R.G. LeTourneau*

This is what changed our ministry while living in Ethiopia. We rarely knew how much financial support would come in each month to support our family and the movement God was raising up in Ethiopia among many of the young leaders and kids we were working with. We could not always plan what the month would look like, but we could listen to the Spirit, be obedient and give liberally with Him each day as provision came in.

We had multiple shelters we opened, lots of discipleship groups, setting the kids up with jobs on the streets, meals for new kids we were meeting, and a growing team. Our incredible friends and ministry partners, John & Terina Dutton and family, moved there to join us for a time in that season and gave unconditionally. There wasn't a measurement of what they needed, rather, they just gave according to how God was leading and trusted Him with us for how He would continue to refill all our tanks. The most fruitful months for our newly arising leadership team and the kids they were working with from the street were months I would look back on and realize that God had us all give between 80-90% of what came in. And yet, we always had enough for our family as well. In fact, God wasn't growing a ministry for us or through us. He was growing a family. Our lives grew more abundant by the day!

Some of our favorite testimonies of God's faithfulness and provision came from those streets of Ethiopia, but not just in how we saw God provide for us. Perhaps the best part was watching the kids who lived on the street, who were immersed in the bondages of poverty and dependence, learn to depend on God more than man or money, and trust Him to show up as their Provider too. They naturally assumed we were rich Americans. And compared to their state of life, we were, and are. But we tried to help them know that despite where we came from or the color of our skin, we didn't have a full bank account either. I think it was hard for them to believe, but through stories and letting them see our faith and trust put to the test, they slowly started to understand that we, too, were living by faith more than by money.

One of the ways we always sought to empower the kids on the street was by teaching them to wait on God in prayer and learn to hear His voice. We taught them what God had taught us, that if you know how to hear God's voice, there's nothing else you could ever need. Because then, if you know God's voice, you know when to go left, and you know when to go right. If you listen for God's voice, then you know when to stop, wait and be patient, and you know when to go and perhaps even leap by faith. If you know how to hear God's voice, backed of course by His word in the Bible, then there is nothing else you could ever need. This is what Jesus Himself said in the wilderness when the devil was trying to tempt Him during His fast. But Jesus responded, "Man does not live by bread alone, but by every word that proceeds from the mouth of God." Notice Jesus didn't just say, "by every word that has proceeded" from the mouth of God, as in past tense. He said it in the present/future tense, that we live by "every word that proceeds," from the mouth of God. As in, God is alive, and still speaking.

When we learn to know God in this way it does two things. One, we simply just get to know Him better. And it is much easier to trust someone that you know well. Two, we learn to depend on God, His word and His voice as our Provider instead of man, money or the world's sources. Essentially, it teaches us to go straight to the real Source!

We would meet the street kids in a park among the streets where they usually begged, and it was there that we would practice waiting on God and hearing His voice together. Then, we would encourage them in how to put this into practice in their daily lives. For instance, many of them had grown up begging each day just to eat, and as their primary, if not the only source of income. They lived and operated in an area where there were lots of tourists, so this was a prime spot for them to beg and depend on men, all the while staying in their current circumstances.

That's where we challenged them. "What if next time you are hungry and tempted to beg, don't go up to a foreigner, but go somewhere quiet by yourself and ask your Heavenly Father instead?" This was breaking their box of everything they had known. But the more they spent time with us in God's presence, the more they started to feel encouraged and strengthened to try. It was our greatest joy when unprompted, they started coming back to our regular meetings with new testimonies.

One came back and told us, "I was hungry the other day and needed food. I was tempted to go and ask and beg from the tourists. Instead, I went away for a few minutes and just asked God. When I came back into the streets, someone came up to me, tapped me on the shoulder and said, 'Can I buy you lunch?'"

The young man was floored! He couldn't believe he saw God answer in such a tangible, timely way.

Or the other boy who said he needed a bike for various work and practical reasons. Instead of begging, or stealing, this time, he said he prayed and asked God for a bike. He could hardly believe God answered his prayers by someone giving him a bike.

And yet another boy who wanted to work instead of begging. But, relatively speaking, there is a lot that goes into setting up a shoe-shining business for a kid living on the street. He went against all his previous patterns and went to the Lord instead. Before he knew it, someone had come and offered to set him up with a full shoe-shining business.

These kids, regardless of poverty, age, or other, simply needed to know the same God we knew. They didn't only need what we could give them or teach them about. They needed to know how to engage with the same Living God who had become our Faithful Provider. He is the same God for them as He is for us—when we allow Him to be!

a creative
miracle

chapter 10
a creative miracle

When I first met "Berhanu" (name changed for privacy), I was overcome with heartache and compassion for his outer condition. In fact, I was so focused on his outer condition that I could have easily missed what God wanted to do inside him. He lived on the streets and was just about to turn fourteen. A lot of kids on the streets have many things in common, but Berhanu faced a challenge few others ever had; he had no arms.

Berhanu's arms had been lost in an accident while he was playing near a railroad track some three years earlier. He had stumps at his shoulders, but a smile that could light up a room. Berhanu started meeting up with the other kids and our team of spiritual fathers and mothers on a regular basis. The first time I met him was at one of our "street church" gatherings. My heart sank as I saw his sleeves drooping down, but my spirits were lifted when I saw the way the other kids interacted with him, especially how they served him so selflessly. I will never forget watching another boy patiently feed Berhanu his breakfast. One bite at a time, the boy tore off a piece of bread and dipped it into the tea, helping him to enjoy both at once. Berhanu sat receiving his breakfast with immense humility and grace, though I had to wonder how this made him feel deep inside—was it a struggle for him to hide his hurt and shame?

One of the ways we empowered the kids on the street was to purchase goods for them to sell, usually a tray full of cookies, tissues, gum and the like. The other most common option was to buy them a shoeshine box. This empowered them to work, and we coupled this with getting them re-started in a local school. Berhanu obviously was less likely to shine shoes—though we did find out he was very adept at utilizing his feet for hands—so we set him up with a tray of goods to sell. As you can imagine, two things happened for Berhanu. One, some people would go above and beyond in their generosity towards him because of his disability, by paying him a little extra tip, or showing him some other kindness to help. The second sort of encounter Berhanu would run into, though, wasn't so friendly: other kids on the street cycling in their own poverty, just waiting to take advantage of him. Not only would they lift the tray that was hung around his neck straight off him for themselves, but they'd also reach into his pockets and steal all his profits, knowing there wasn't a thing about it he could do. This occurrence didn't need to happen much for us to realize that something had to be done.

We were in the middle of setting up the first street shelter where the boys would live, but it was still going to take a few more weeks before it was ready. We paid for the other kids to stay each night in a local shelter, but this wouldn't work anymore for Berhanu. He needed a different answer, an answer God now asked us to provide.

Like many of the kids on the streets, Berhanu did have a family living in the countryside. Also, like many of the other kids, the extreme poverty they lived in caused huge rifts in the home, stirring up various forms of abuse, irrational fights, lack of food or opportunity, and a greatly impoverished hope. This lack of hope is why most of the kids leave home actually, even the ones who still have a good family—they go into the city searching for a glimmer of hope. Berhanu had a father and mother at home who loved him, and several siblings as well. But he battled all those things that many of the other kids battled, with one huge extra: His lack of arms brought on even greater discouragement and depression, not to mention bullying from the other kids in his village. He wanted nothing—and I mean nothing—to do with going home. He didn't want to make a phone call, or even talk about his family. It was a gaping wound that left a huge hole in his life, more so even than his arms.

We knew that until the street shelter was ready, and because he was unwilling to go back to his family, we needed to welcome Berhanu to live with us. Mind you, this wasn't any kind of a rash emotional decision, nor were we trying to be heroes. It was simple obedience. We had only a short time to decide, needing to remove him from the extra vulnerability he was experiencing on the streets. But we also needed to pray. We had to make sure that it was God's idea and not just ours. This was not a decision to be taken lightly. We had four daughters at home and were looking at welcoming in a fourteen-year-old boy from the streets. It was a very serious situation. God was gracious to give us several confirmations and wisdom regarding how to set up our home and his time with us. We also met with the other street kids first to explain the situation, not wanting any of them to feel left out or that Berhanu was being given preference. We wanted them to understand the circumstances he was battling. Truth be told, they knew his battles far better than we did. They were very gracious and understanding—at least most of them—and wanted what was best for Berhanu. It was a proud moment seeing their responses of love towards him, even though they knew they weren't the ones coming to live with us.

So, we invited Berhanu to our home, letting him know he would be considered part of the family and could stay with us until the shelter was ready for him. He was thrilled to take us up on our offer and arrived swiftly to join us. We began to learn a lot about Berhanu, which was easy because he spoke English well compared to most of the kids. His English proficiency stemmed from one of those surprising nuggets he let us in on. See, Berhanu may have only been fourteen, and he may have been living on the streets, but he had also been to America. Yes, you read that right. Berhanu had been to America! We were shocked, too! He began to tell us all about it and then even went so far as to show us evidence of his time in the U.S., the family he had lived with for months, and the goal of his visit, which was to receive a prosthetic arm—a very expensive, technologically built arm.

Obviously, we weren't the first to meet Berhanu and take notice. But what dropped our jaws—and our hearts—even more was the fact that afterwards, he was right back out on the streets. The family, the doctors and so many others who had loved him so well had no idea, either. As far as they knew, Berhanu had returned to a great family situation. He should have been flourishing with his new technological limb after having been given the gift of a lifetime. Unfortunately, that's not what happened, and there was no way for this generous family, who obviously loved him so much, to know that Berhanu had returned immediately to his old cycle of poverty. All the while, his new prosthetic arm sat at his family's home unused, worth more than his family would typically earn over years and years combined. This realization left us heartbroken, seeing the grip that poverty has on the inside, even while external needs are generously and extravagantly fulfilled.

I don't share this at all to indict the family who supplied this gift to Berhanu.

Their intentions and giving were through the roof. His story is simply a sad portrayal of the secret life of poverty and how it slithers about to keep its grip on lives from the inside, waiting for us to feed it further. We were still intending to love Berhanu in a way like that of the previous family, largely focused on addressing his outer poverty. We were praying for new arms for him, too! And when I say this, I understand that many people have a different take on miracles and whether they still occur today. We do believe that miracles do still occur today. I have been an active recipient and participant too many times not to believe. We've watched Biblical-sized miracles happen before our eyes; we've seen growths disappear and a foot healed, and we know many others who have witnessed far more. I had known of stories from great friends who have witnessed missing limbs, such as Berhanu's being re-grown. Believing this way, why would we not begin asking the Father for new arms for Berhanu? Sure, it might sound a little crazy, but the least we could do is ask, and believe. Our Father is good like that.

But the purpose of this story is not to convince you of miracles. I simply want you to understand where we were initially coming from in addressing Berhanu's poverty and lack. There are many ways in which we good-heartedly address external needs. Just as his first family from America had, we focused on his outward circumstances and hoped to see some form of healing. The simple fact that Berhanu had his needs met with such abundance and yet still ended up away from his family and back on the streets without his new arm reminds us that there is a deeper level of poverty God wants to address through us—the healing of hearts.

As we prayed for Berhanu's arms to be restored, as well as for other needs in his life to be met, the Lord reminded me of the compassion that often-preceded Jesus' miracles. However, I know this isn't a superficial kind of compassion that is "feelings" or "emotions" oriented. It's the kind of compassion that can bear a burden from a deep core of understanding what someone else is going through. It was then, in response to those prayers asking the Lord to teach me such compassion for Berhanu, that God put a challenge before me: "How can you know what Berhanu truly goes through if you have not experienced such yourself?" And you know what? He was right. Imagine that! I had seen but didn't fully know the kind of suffering Berhanu battled each day, but I was committed to understanding. I needed to understand at a deeper level so that I could know even better how to pray. It was clear what I had to do. I would live for twenty-four hours without using my arms, having them bandaged to my body so I couldn't cheat even once.

Let me start out by saying that my plan of "going without arms for a day" wasn't as simple as it may sound. I have had several broken arms and serious shoulder injuries that required my arm to be immobilized and pressed against my chest for weeks. Even one day of this was completely different! We rely on our arms and their natural presence far more than we realize for things such as balance and other functions we may take for granted. Also, before I could go through with my plan, there were two people I had to bring in on the decision: First, I needed to ask my wife's permission, because, as you can probably imagine, there would be a lot I would need her help for—a lot! Once Destiny had graciously given approval to her vital part in this (her part may even have been harder than mine), then I needed to share with Berhanu some of what was going on in our hearts. We wanted to honor him in every bit of this, not just from our perspective, but from his as well. We didn't focus on the "new arms" we were praying for as much as we let him know that we believed God wanted to do a greater work in his life, and we wanted to join in. I made it very clear that this was not funny to me; it was not a joke, but something I took very seriously because of his value to us, and to God. Berhanu was very receptive, smiled about it, and, truth be told, couldn't wait for me to begin. I think he was genuinely blessed and looked forward to someone understanding even one percent of the reality of his life. We finished the planning and made sure that my twenty-four-hour span would include a busy day full of responsibilities for me. If I were to be just sitting around the house, I'd only get a measure of what I could learn. It had to happen on one of my peak days.

I decided to start the clock at about 10 pm, knowing I'd have to go through one night of sleep in total. For me, that sleep was one of the most challenging parts of the whole twenty-four hours. I was miserably uncomfortable all night, having forgotten just how much I move and position my arms even at night for comfort. To have them strapped down felt torturous—and that was just while sleeping!

I won't go through the whole twenty-four hours with you, but let's just say there were a lot of challenges in what we consider menial day-to-day activities, things we take for granted; like eating, showering, or going to the bathroom. It was extremely difficult to be forced to constantly receive help in these humbling ways. Also, I was used to being driven by ideas, hopes, vision and purpose. But now, suddenly, my opportunities felt limited. My situation discouraged my hope much more quickly than I anticipated. There was less I could dream to do, and little I could start or finish on my own. I didn't know where to begin. That's when I really started to understand Berhanu's poverty—not just understanding him through knowledge with my mind—but with my heart. I felt his plight, and the places where identity took a beating. I felt the tiniest touch of the pounding his heart must take from things like shame and hopelessness. It is discouraging to continually be dependent on someone else, even for the tiniest of life's minute details. There is a lot of discontent, and the poisons of hope deferred try to inject themselves quickly when you feel so restricted in dreams and possibilities. I mean, I couldn't even go to the bathroom by myself, let alone figure out some of the more purposeful things I wanted to get started on.

These limitations may seem easy to overcome, but they can be crushing to a heart and force someone into deeper levels of poverty than our eyes ever see. That's when it hit me. The Lord had given me exactly what I had asked for through these twenty-four hours without arms. He showed me a different perspective of Berhanu's healing. Berhanu didn't need new arms as much as he first needed a new heart! God could give him new arms any day of the week, but He was a Father broken over the internal and unseen wounds of his young son, looking for someone who would embrace the mission field that consisted of the cracks and bruises of his heart. We could now see what we were only partially aware of before. This kind of heart healing goes beyond someone repeating a prayer of external words for salvation (which Berhanu had already done), and truly allows the Lord's love to come in and speak life over what poverty and hope deferred had tried to destroy.

I took this back to the Lord in prayer to ask for His strategy: "Father, how do You want to give Berhanu a new heart?" He led me to a passage in the book of Ezekiel that I still hold onto for strategy today:

"I will give you a new heart and put a new spirit within you; I will take the heart of stone out of your flesh and give you a heart of flesh. I will put My Spirit within you and cause you to walk in My statutes, and you will keep My judgments and do them. Then you shall dwell in the land that I gave to your fathers; you shall be My people, and I will be your God.

"I will deliver you from all your uncleannesses. I will call for the grain and multiply it, and bring no famine upon you. And I will multiply the fruit of your trees and the increase of your fields, so that you need never again bear the reproach of famine among the nations. . . ."

'Thus says the Lord God: "On the day that I cleanse you from all your iniquities, I will also enable you to dwell in the cities, and the ruins shall be rebuilt. The desolate land shall be tilled instead of lying desolate in the sight of all who pass by. So they will say, 'This land that was desolate has become like the garden of Eden; and the wasted, desolate, and ruined cities are now fortified and inhabited.' Then the nations which are left all around you shall know that I, the Lord, have rebuilt the ruined places and planted what was desolate. I, the Lord, have spoken it, and I will do it." (Ezekiel 36: 26-30, 33-36)

What a conclusion to the passage! "I will do it," says the Lord. And with Berhanu, He certainly did. It wasn't our ways of mission that brought transformation to Berhanu's life; it was God's supernatural gift of a new heart. To me, this passage became such an inspiring picture of multiplication. Multiplication starts with one heart being healed of true poverty. This brings a new spirit, cleaned of the old wounds that plagued it as the engine behind poverty's cycle and free to transform from that new heart into a land that is no longer desolate, but so fruitful it becomes once again like the Garden of Eden. This is what I believe now for every life we address in poverty; each in its own unique way. We saw it happen firsthand in and through Berhanu, who taught us so much about the levels of poverty people battle.

With Berhanu, we took this passage literally, believing that God wanted to bring it to life in his heart. I went to several of our local team members and to our family and shared further what the Lord had shared with me. We thought we needed to have a time of prayer over Berhanu and lay hands on him together, showering him with love and praying for God's new heart in his life to replace the wounded one poverty had bludgeoned. I asked Berhanu if he would be open to receiving this ministry. He agreed, and we all gathered one afternoon in our living room to believe God for Berhanu's new heart. It was a powerful time of prayer. God's presence and love were palpable, and though we couldn't see any physical changes with our eyes, we knew the Father had gone to work in Berhanu's heart.

The next day Berhanu came to me and asked if it would be okay for him to call his parents. I was completely surprised and almost didn't know what to say. I actually questioned him because of the sheer amount of stubbornness he had always shown in everything relating to his home and family. But now he was coming to us, the very day after God had set us on His mission towards Berhanu's broken heart. He called home and had a very good conversation with his mom. The next day Berhanu came to us yet again with a new request that almost worried us at first: "I'm ready to go home to my family. Can you take me home now?" Whoa! Again, we questioned him to make sure he was ready, trying to figure out how he could change from one strong opinion to the opposite so rapidly. Was he truly prepared for such a drastic change already? We didn't want him to rush into it and cause more problems again. But Berhanu was certain in his stance, and we were not about to stand in the way of what God was doing. It was such a vivid portrayal of part of that Ezekiel 36 passage: *"On the day that I cleanse you from all your iniquities, I will also enable you to dwell in the cities, and the ruins shall be rebuilt."* God had done this for Berhanu just as He said He would. Rome may not be built in a day, but God can heal any heart of even great depths of poverty in but one short day.

Berhanu returned home accompanied by a couple of members of our team of spiritual fathers and mothers. They built a relationship with his family the same way we built one with Berhanu. The team would not only visit with Berhanu like they once did on the streets, but now, they were also visiting his whole family with the same love and care. Now that is multiplication! God took the heart He healed in Berhanu and began to spread that same healing to his whole family. Before we knew it, Berhanu's family was able to move into a new home, started taking new steps forward in life, and even began reaching out to other distant family members in other parts of the country. Berhanu's new heart, just as the passage laid out, led to a desolate land being made fruitful again. And for the remaining years of his adolescence, Berhanu never ran away from home again. For the first time, the restlessness of his pain and lack of hope didn't drive him away. God healed Berhanu's poverty through a miracle that was different than where we had begun, and different from where we usually expect.

coming back from ethiopia

chapter 11
coming back from ethiopia

When we left Ethiopia it was one of the hardest decisions we ever made, and even harder to go through with. We had truly built a home, and a family there. The Lord had birthed a statement in our hearts while there, "When you minister to someone, they might get loved, but when you love them, they always get ministered to."

Our time in Ethiopia was not about ministry, it was about building, growing and redeeming God's family. That meant we had to learn to love them like family. And each day we did our best to do just that; to give them and love them with all that we had.

Even the process of leaving was difficult to discern at first. We anguished in prayer for weeks. We hadn't planned to leave after three years, yet so much of our focus there was empowering locals, and the longer we were there we were concerned that we might breed more dependence on us instead of handing them the baton and letting them learn to run, lead and multiply on their own.

Also, we always felt such grace over each part of our family while we were there, even in the hardest moments, we knew we had a grace to navigate through those days and seasons. But it started to feel like that grace was starting to lift a little bit. We were starting to feel subtle little ways that our kids were feeling the effects in ways that hadn't been before. And with our adoption of Ayni and Anna (formerly Kelemua), it was starting to feel important for somewhat of a "leave and cleave" season for them outside the culture there (as much as we love the culture there!) and establish a new foundation for them out of our family culture apart from Ethiopia. That said, we couldn't get a clear word from the Lord on whether to stay, or go. All we wanted was to be in fresh, obedient alignment with the Lord; not staying too long, not leaving too early.

Finally, I was up on the roof of our second house we rented in Ethiopia, just for our last six months there. It had a flat roof with an apartment and was a tall, narrow four-story building. It became one of my favorite places to seek the Lord, listen, worship and pray over the city and the generation we were praying forward there.

Still asking the Lord for a clear answer, one day I looked around and saw the clouds moving in quickly. The wind was blowing and you could tell a storm was likely on its way. As I noticed this, I was reminded of the verses in Matthew 16 when the Pharisees and Sadducees were asking Jesus for a sign:

"He answered and said to them, "When it is evening, you say, 'It will be fair weather, for the sky is red'; 'and in the morning, 'It will be foul weather today, for the sky is red and threatening.' 'Hypocrites! You know how to discern the face of the sky, but you cannot discern the signs of the times.'" (Matthew 16:2-3)

I realized I too was asking the Lord for a clear sign of whether to stay or to go. But what I was failing to do was to discern the clouds and skies of our family, our mission, and other aspects of our lives and season that the Lord had put in front of us. As we all often do, I wanted clarity in a black-and-white sense. But that is almost never what walking by faith is. It is usually a discerning of the Spirit's movement, and His invitation for us to join Him. God doesn't force Himself upon us, but He gives us bread crumbs we can pick up. He shows us a cloud with one member of our family, or a gust of wind around another. He waits for us to stop always asking for a clear sign but instead to recognize the small, subtle changes in the "weather" of our lives and families.

As I realized this that day, I knew we had our answer. It was time to leave our home in Ethiopia and move our family back to the States. I could see the answer we had been waiting for written across each member of our family, myself included, in different ways. And once we recognized how the Lord had already been speaking, immense peace covered us as we navigated the challenge of leaving our Ethiopian family and home.

a new home

When we finally arrived back in the States, we landed in Colorado, where we planned to set up our home base once again. Thankfully, we had some close friends who offered for us to stay with them for the first number of weeks as we got settled. We really needed the time to unwind, and unfortunately got very sick which forced us to really lay low and rest for longer than we otherwise would have. They also had a van for us to borrow, just big enough for our then family of six (we're a family of 10 now!) God's grace was all over our return in these ways which helped confirm the steps we had taken with the move—especially with how hard it was to leave.

As we started to settle in it became time to figure out what our home and life would look like now. The area we were coming back to was one of the fastest growing and more expensive counties in the nation. And we still did not have any guaranteed salary to prove income for a new place to live.

Up until our move to Ethiopia, we had always lived in apartments because when we left, it had just been Destiny, Mercy and I, but now we were coming back with Destiny and I and four amazing girls. We knew we needed a house, and that would be more expensive rent than anything we had ventured into before. Truly, we had no way to even set a clear budget with where our monthly income was at or what we could afford. All we had, as usual for us, was the ability to pray, listen for how or where to step, and then trust God to make a way.

We kept searching for houses in Parker, CO, where I had grown up and where we were married, and Mercy was born. By faith, we set an amount we knew might be a stretch; because truth be told it was several hundred dollars per month more than we had ever paid for rent. But we couldn't find anything in that range.

There was one house however that kept popping up. It was a little older, but in a neighborhood we had always loved! It didn't seem feasible for our situation, and the rent was about $400 more than the amount we already thought would be a stretch. However, we really felt the Lord's light over it like no other house we found, so we went to look at it anyway.

The home was being rented through an agency; thus, it had a fairly extensive application process. And it sounded like there were quite a few interested, and already a handful of applications were submitted. We wanted this house so bad, felt God's light and grace over it, and yet even though we were stepping by faith towards any home, we still wanted to be responsible as well. We called the agency and asked a few more questions, the most important of which, to us anyway, was if they would be willing to come down on rent at all, seeing as it was so much more beyond even our "faith budget." They marked it down another $50, but that was as far as they could go.

At that point, we were trying so hard to be "responsible" that we started to decide based on our reasoning rather than on the Lord's direction, or faith. So, we told them thank you, but no thank you and moved on from that home. Within a day, we were growing very uncomfortable with our answer. We called the rental agency to inquire again, but this time they said the house had now been rented and was under contract. We were so bummed!

After saying no, and hearing that the house was under contract, we were very restless in our spirits. We felt like we missed out on something. It wasn't just conviction, that is often more geared for when you've done something wrong. No, this was more about not taking a step forward or open door that God wanted to lead us through. None of the other houses felt right. They could have been bigger, for cheaper, and it still wouldn't have mattered as that house just felt like it had a light over it from the Lord for us.

Destiny and I talked about it and decided we needed to go by the house again and pray. We drove up and pulled into the driveway.

"Lord, please forgive us. We repent of our not trusting you for more. We repent of not stepping towards the place You were highlighting for us. Please give us another chance. In Jesus' name, Amen."

Then we started the car and drove away. Nothing else happened at that moment, no phone call to the agency, just repenting for our lack of faith forward with the Lord. It wasn't long after that though that the phone rang. It was the rental agency for the house. They said that the other contract had just suddenly fallen through, and the house was open for application again. "Wow, thank You, God," we celebrated! We didn't want to miss our chance again. So, this time, we weren't going to let price be the dictating factor, rather, God had to be the dictating factor.

We pulled up again to the home to meet them and fill out an application. They did tell us however that there were at least four other applications being considered. As you can imagine, this made us very nervous seeing as our application and proof of income did not exactly match up with all the specific qualifications. But this wasn't about qualifications, this was about us doing our part, obediently stepping out on God's nudge, and then trusting Him to show up on our behalf.

As good as we knew God to be, as faithful as we had seen Him show up with us or on our behalf, we still were amazed when we got the call that the agency and owners had chosen us out of all the applicants. We may not have matched up on paper, but as Isaiah 55 reminds us, God's ways are higher than our ways, and His thoughts higher than our thoughts.

He doesn't change. He and His ways are always that much higher. Unfortunately, we often try and live below the cloud line, underneath the cloud-like weight of man's reason, all the while, God is beckoning us to accept His invitation to rise higher, and step forward with Him into the new thing He wants to do.

"Do not remember the former things, nor consider the things of old. Behold, I will do a new thing, now it shall spring forth; Shall you not know it?" (Isaiah 43:18-19)

learning

abundance

chapter 12
learning abundance

We made a lot of memories living in that house God set us up when we came back from Ethiopia. Like many of our stops, we were only there a short time, two years to be exact. A lot started with the publishing of our book, _Revolutionary Freedom_, that I mentioned earlier, and then a couple of other books to follow with that same publisher during that time. It was there that I finished writing, _The Life Giver_, and we started traveling stateside a good bit to share about the book and to speak to different groups.

The theme of _The Life Giver_ is John 10:10, "The thief does not come but to steal, kill, and destroy, but I have come that you might have life and have it in abundance." It's clear that there is an eternal emphasis there, but it is very relevant for us during our time here on Earth as well. That said, we were fully aware that we had not yet had "earthly abundance" in a monetary sense, and God was using that teaching us to live by faith rather than by what we have in our hands, or what we can control. I also know that "abundance" is defined very differently according to God's perspective versus man's.

Abundantly comes from "Perissos": "Superabundance, excessive, overflowing, surplus, over and above, more than enough, profuse, extraordinary, above the ordinary, more than sufficient."

Typically, people hear abundance and simply think of having a lot of material goods. And while that is certainly a part of abundance, there is a different level of wealth, or fullness, that is represented in kingdom abundance. I started to realize more and more the depths and layers of what an "abundant mindset" might mean. We are created to desire life more abundantly, but too often pursue a counterfeit version. Abundantly is the way God's Kingdom does life, and we're called to fill our abundant cravings not just by content discipline, but with discontent faith! We reach for external excess and spoil the concept of abundant living and create an over-spiritualized version of life that makes sacrifice the focus rather than the product. To live abundantly is to have unquenchable faith while freely receiving, and freely giving out unmerited favor and undeserved blessings. Jesus lived every day of His life in abundance, while never relying upon the abundance in His hands.

Often, we want to wait for promises such as those of abundance or wealth to come to us. In a sense, they do. But usually in a more internal, hidden way that lets such promise grow in us first, and then come to life through us.

True Abundance is a mindset and heart-full, a place of fullness even in the midst of apparent lack. Paul perhaps alludes to it best in Philippians 4:11-13: *"Not that I speak in regard to need, for I have learned in whatever state I am to be content: I know how to be abased, and I know how to abound. Everywhere and in all things I have learned both to be full and to be hungry, both to abound and to suffer need. I can do all things through Christ who strengthens me."*

The last part of that verse is quoted a lot. In fact, it was one of my favorites growing up. But I hadn't begun to taste of its depth or fullness yet (and probably still haven't). Paul wants everyone to know that no matter what was going on in the natural, he was full. He was surrendered to a different kind of fullness that wasn't defined merely by externals. I call this true abundance because he has it at a level that is defined by God rather than by man. Our ability to transition to this kind of genuine belief and contentment, relaxed, surrendered, and not worried no matter what state or pressure we are in, prepares us to walk in true abundance. It breaks off worry and fear. It breaks abundance out of being defined (confined) by money alone and recognizes that true abundance is something inside us before it's in our hands; and how important that is as part of our preparation for such.

During this season, we wanted to press into the Lord and learn more about His perspective of abundance. We wanted to understand how to steward abundance. We wanted to live with an abundant mindset. And most of this goes beyond managing a ledger of a surplus of cash. So, we decided to commit to the Lord that we would give the next 40 days to learning abundance, having no idea what that might mean, nor what we were in for!

As we've shared through many stories and seasons already, we have often lived by faith day-to-day as far as provision goes; not knowing when, how or how much would come in. Some days, weeks, or months could get very tight, but God has always been more than faithful in the smallest and biggest of ways. But what happened at the start of this "40 days of abundance" was on a different level. Almost immediately, our account dropped to zero without any checks coming in to replenish it. Within a day or two, it was overdrawn to the tune of negative two hundred dollars. And still, no checks were coming in. But while our natural account said zero, every day, God kept finding new ways to provide for us. On top of it all, during that first half of the forty days of abundance, we were hosting two different families of 6+ people each at different times and hosting a Thanksgiving meal at our house. But through all of that, the bottom of our barrel never ran out. God brought different vehicles of grace, and fresh manna every day. He filled our pantry, had unaware neighbors bringing over pans of high-end steak dinners, and somehow put together a massive Thanksgiving feast and blessed all our time with company those first twenty days! And most of that while our account stayed in the negative. But "negative" didn't define how we were living. Our account said one thing, but each day, God said or showed something else. As much as it didn't look like we had any earthly "abundance," we were living abundantly out of heaven's resources every day in a way that only God could orchestrate.

Then, right at the halfway point, we were hitting a moment with some bigger bills due, a couple of needs that were put off were now rounding back, and we very much needed a financial breakthrough of a different sort. We were praying and thanking God for His abundance, trusting that just as He provided over the past twenty days, He would be just as faithful for the rest. But that night, we were starting to feel the pressure a little bit. That's part of the reality of walking by faith; you often very much feel the reality of the storm around you or the uncertainty under your feet, the faith part comes in with what you do with or through those realities. I was sitting at my desk trying to figure a few things out when our daughter, Galilee, asked if I'd come to play a board game with her. It was a word game of some sort that I wasn't familiar with, and truth be told I wasn't at all in the mood to play a game. But I felt the Holy

Spirit nudging me, reminding me to not let the pressures I was starting to feel dictate to my attitude, our family, or the atmosphere of our home. So, maybe a board game with her was exactly what I needed.

We started to play and when my turn rolled around, the first word card that I drew was "GRATE." Then, when it was my turn again, interestingly, the card I picked up was the word, "PROVISION." Huh, I thought that was kind of coincidental, considering the season we were in and what we were praying for that day. But I still didn't think much of it. That is, until my next card came up. My next card I picked up was the word, "ENTER." And suddenly, I was putting the pieces together. My cards read, "GRATE PROVISION ENTER." Now that's a game I could get on board with, I thought, finding it both amusing and hopeful at the same time.

We finished our game, and I held onto my cards, as it felt almost like a prayer or declaration to agree with, may "GRATE PROVISION ENTER." And as wild as it sounds, within about fifteen minutes of that lineup of cards, we got an unexpected phone call from some friends in another state. They had been praying and felt the Lord wanted them to send us a donation of $10,000. It was more than enough to cover the mounting bills and needs and gave us a monetary abundance to live from that we hadn't had in some time. We went from the first twenty days seeing God provide abundantly even when it seemed we were in lack, and then, in the second half of those forty days our account was overflowing according to our current standards.

But you know what, God was teaching us about true abundance through both of those ways. Our circumstance, whether abased or abounding, didn't define abundance. Rather, it was God's form of abundance that defined our circumstances. He wanted us to know, and experience the truth that we could live abundantly in both realities. We were content and had more than enough during the first twenty days, and we were content and had more than enough during the next twenty days. Like Paul, in every situation, we were full and/or overflowing. *That, is true abundance!*

to
california
again

chapter 13

to california again

We had been back living in Colorado for about three and half years when the Lord started to impress upon our hearts a call to head back towards California, specifically to Redding, CA. I had a specific dream involving Redding, and even more so, a series of whispers from God's still, small voice and confirmations to back them up. The problem, however, was that we were still bound to a large, intricate lease in our current house and had bills piling up in a tight season once again.

We have found that often, not always, but often a season will get tighter financially when the grace is lifting and we're supposed to transition forward in some new way, or to some new place. This was certainly the case in this situation. Honestly, the thought of trying to move in our current circumstances felt impossible.

We called the owners of the house to ask about prematurely ending the lease, but that door was firmly sealed to the contract, and if we broke it without finding new tenants, we would still owe roughly $18,000. On top of that, we had a couple thousand dollars more that had piled up in bills, and very little daily income coming in. But we continued to feel God leading and confirming the move out west. We hadn't even factored in moving costs yet, a large moving truck for a family of six and approval into a new home in Redding being the largest of the obstacles. We continued to pray and make sure this wasn't an "us" thing, that it was God's idea and not just ours. The more we prayed, the more convinced we were. So, despite the needs and the many mountains to be moved, by faith, we gave our notice to the house owners of breaking the lease and the date the Lord had given us to move by.

The move date was just under two months out, so the first thing we did was start to look for a new renter. This was not an easy task. If we were going to leave, the owner wanted to increase the price by another couple hundred dollars per month, as well as be very specific as to who was and wasn't allowed to see the home as far as qualifications go. We had to make sure not to look at the mounting impossibilities because things certainly weren't moving yet.

At the same time, we were having a hard time finding many good housing options that fit our family out in Redding. Not to mention, once again, how we would qualify for another new place and get approved. With every move, we had to find where God's grace was at for that season. If we went by typical methods, our particulars still just didn't match up to most rental applications. But when we found the right grace, God was leading us to—whether people, timing, specific location, etc.—God's provision and straightened path always followed. We also recognized that the van we had been given upon arriving back in Colorado was now on its last legs. We had used it those three and a half years for many more faith road trips, crossing many miracle lines, but it would not make another move across the country—that much was sure.

The build-up to our moving date was a real battle. Keeping our eyes off the numbers, and away from the stormy realities all around, we just kept moving forward. For us, it's often much like the Jordan River story where the river was not parted until their feet first went into the water. There are moments when you wait patiently for the Lord to move, and moments where you keep moving forward regardless. It takes both faith and patience to inherit God's promises in each season (Hebrews 6:12)

Thankfully, God gave us a specific passage of scripture when we first started to feel His leading on the move:

"For you shall go out with joy, and be led out with peace; the mountains and the hills shall break forth into singing before you, and all the trees of the field shall clap their hands. Instead of the thorn shall come up the cypress tree, and instead of the brier shall come up the myrtle tree; and it shall be to the Lord for a name, for an everlasting sign that shall not be cut off." (Isaiah 55:12-13)

This passage got us through so many of those days, starting the moving process when nothing was moving forward yet. God spoke it over our move so clearly that when reality told us one thing, we just held onto, prayed and declared that verse that told us another. We lived off that promise for weeks, believing it would come to pass.

We were only a couple weeks now from our moving date and nothing—and I mean NOTHING—had happened yet. It was the exact opposite of what we were hearing from the Lord. And different than many of our other moves as well. But one Sunday night, half discouraged, and half believing, I sat up late in a chair in our living room, just trying to be still with the Lord. That's when a still, small voice blew in over my shoulder, catching me completely off guard. "Get ready to run," I heard clearly. "Huh!" What did that even mean? We've been trying to and absolutely nothing was coming together. But almost like the halfway point in our 40 days of Abundance, it felt like the Lord was saying that things were about to shift dramatically, and we had to be prepared to ride that wave.

Immediately the next day, things started moving. And I don't mean just a little bit. Suddenly we were getting good, potential calls and visits on the house, provision started to come in to catch up on the other ways we were in the red, and God highlighted one house for rent in Redding that we felt like we were supposed to pursue. Everything started to move so fast, no wonder God had told us to "get ready to run." It was almost comical. We found a new tenant for the house whom the owner agreed upon, so the debt on our lease was wiped out. We began discussions with the house owners out in Redding, we reserved a rental van to make the move with and booked the moving truck to pick up the morning of our moving date, though we still did not yet have the funds necessary to pay for the truck.

The process with the house in Redding was active, but slow. We tried to explain our situation but weren't sure if we were going to be approved or not. Do we make the move anyway? What if we have nowhere to land? All the different questions start to come up, but we felt like God was setting up this specific house for us, so we just kept moving forward.

It was the day before our move, and we still didn't have the thousand-plus dollars to pick up our Penske truck in less than 24 hours. Neither did we have the house in Redding fully agreed upon. Oddly, that morning I got a call from a close friend who lives in Redding, but he happened to be in Colorado, of all places and was passing through our small town and wondered if I had time last minute to meet for coffee. This friend was like a brother, so even though we were in the wild throws of moving, I couldn't pass up getting a few minutes to catch up and talk Jesus together, as we always spurred one another on.

He loved hearing our faith stories over the years and was asking all about this move, excited that we were going to be near him for the coming season. I shared all the twists and turns, the obstacles, the miracles, and the specific words the Lord had given us. Suddenly his eyes lit up:

"Joey, I'm so sorry I almost forgot, a couple weeks ago I felt the Lord tell me I was supposed to pay for your moving truck. When do you pick it up?"

I laughed a laugh of both irony and thankfulness, shaking my head in (almost) disbelief. "Well," I said, in about twenty hours and we weren't sure how we were going to pay for it yet, only that we knew God would provide."

Now we were both laughing. And praising God for His timing and goodness.

The next morning, we woke up and picked up the truck, fully paid for it, and started the immense loading process, packing both the truck and the van until they were both overflowing. Neither could have held much more, our friends came around us and none of us could fit another thing in either vehicle. I'm still not sure how the dogs and all the kids fit in the van with all that was stuffed into every crevice. Meanwhile, the truck had our entire household in it, but we still had not gotten approval on the house in Redding. It wasn't until we literally started driving the truck that we received the word that our application had been accepted, and we were welcome to arrive at our new home in Redding.

Upon arriving in Redding, there were a number of projects and endeavors we had been working on that started to click into place. It's funny, one of those things involved a trip back to Colorado to speak at a Missions Conference barely two weeks after we had moved to California. It felt like one of those times where God was waiting for us to step into right alignment with Him before our new season could take off and promises would start bearing fruit. We rented a van as a long-term rental for a couple of months, funny enough, it ended up being the exact same van that we had just left behind in Colorado. But we were still praying for a long-term vehicle solution for our family. Our first son, Joseph William LeTourneau V, was born shortly before we made this move and little did we know at the time that we would soon have another daughter on the way, Aliyah. We now had six amazing children, who you'll meet more in later testimonies.

The mission conference went amazingly well on multiple levels. I had a great connect with the leadership and the participants and was able to present some of the new things God had given us, resources that help empower people within missions. One man approached me after one of the sessions. He had been in business for many years, largely manufacturing in China working for high-end operations. He loved what I had presented that day and wanted to meet about it further and discuss partnership.

It's funny, that resource was one of the main things on our plate when we had the dream about moving out to Redding and God's new season out there. Yet, this potential business partner was back in Colorado, where we had just moved from. What that always reminds me is that with God, He's more concerned with our alignment with Him than about the logistics of our answered promises. To a person's mind, it would seem to make more sense for that partnership to start before we left Colorado. But perhaps we would have been tempted not to go then. I believe God wanted to align us in the right place for that next season, which then opened the door for the next steps of partnership and forward movement to begin as well.

This businessman, Ernie, was as genuine as could be and had a huge heart for the Lord, and for missions. He flew out to Redding, and we had a series of great meetings about what a partnership might look like. God used that partnership to provide the new (used) Suburban our family needed, and to launch much of the season as to why we had gone to Redding in the first place, as Ernie had the contacts to put our special resource into manufacturing and make it a reality.

Sometimes the answers we're waiting for are actually waiting for us—we just have to step forward to find them. I love Proverbs 25:2, where it says, *"It's the glory of God to conceal a matter, but the glory of kings is to search out a matter."* God hides things not to keep good things from us, but to lead us into even more than we can think or imagine. He draws us out of our comfort zone and invites us to join His process. As people, we are typically more about the end we are searching or waiting for, but God is much more about the means. See, the means, or process, often has as much or even more fruit than the end that we would have settled for. And we don't even see the half of it!

There's much more to that story thereafter, but the point is that God is often waiting on us so He can take us past the very things that we think are making us stuck in the first place. If we will go, if we will step—and keep stepping—He will make a way and lead us past our own plans and into His.

By the end of that move, and even on the drive through the mountains leaving Colorado, we were able to see that promise He gave us from Isaiah 55:12-13 come to life. Truly, He led us out with joy, with peace, and we drove through the fall colors of those rocky mountain trees clapping their hands in the wind. The thorns and briers that threatened us at the outset of the move were no more and had been replaced by the cypress and the myrtle trees instead! God's word never returns void, we can live on it—and move on it as well!

to

israel

chapter 14
to israel

Before leaving Ethiopia, as that door was closing, we felt God start to open a window to a long hoped for promise: Israel. It was so clear one day in prayer. While I had asked God to go, or when we would get to go, many times, this was the first time I felt like I could see it start to open up for us.

When I was eighteen, I felt like I heard the Lord say that in my thirties to forties, I would live in Israel in a strategic, and potentially intense time in the world. Now, we had just moved back to the States a month before my thirtieth birthday. Nothing was planned or on the table yet as far as a trip to Israel, but it felt like God was starting to make a way. And indeed, He was. A couple of new friendships started to form through a rabbit trail of connections stemming from the books we had just published. And in 2014, just after my thirty-third birthday, Destiny, our seven-month-old son, William, and I would be off for our first adventure in Israel.

That trip was a faith trip as we really didn't have any formal hosts to show us around, nor a tour that we were a part of. We had a family-run guesthouse some friends had connected us to, and another meeting to connect with some prayer and prophetic leaders there for the first time. Without going into details of that trip, it became a setup for much more to come. And it started to bring to life some of the other words God had given us before we left Ethiopia as well.

One of those words came when God grabbed my attention one day shortly after finishing our "street church" gathering in Addis Ababa. We had just arrived home, and I was exhausted. I vividly remember setting my Bible down, but as I did, the Lord spoke to me as clearly as I've ever heard Him. *"Pick it back up, I have something for you."* I quickly turned my full attention to Him, "What is it, Lord?"

"Ruth 2," He said

"Ruth 2?!" I questioned back. I wasn't actually questioning Him but was both surprised and curious as to what God had hidden in this familiar story.

"What do you want me to do with it, Lord?" I asked.

"Magnify it," He responded.

This word from the Lord was so clear, it stuck in my spirit and caused me to spend many hours and days asking God how we were to "magnify" Ruth and Boaz and this "Family" redemption story. Some of our answers started to become clear, but another big part of it was something that we couldn't see—yet.

That first trip to Israel was powerful on many levels, as well as strategic. The people we met became close friends, who then also connected us to others in the country as well. One of those new connections was a woman from the U.K., Mary Jane, who had been working in Israel with at-risk youth and families for years and shared a lot of our vision for how to empower them. Also, despite her and our love for Israel and the Jewish people, we also connected on our love for the Palestinian people as well and how to love them the way Jesus would.

Then, in Redding, we soon met a couple who led the Israel trips and ministry for Bethel Church, not just for touring, but to connect with many different ministries in Israel. They really resonated with what we felt called to over there, as well as with some of the resources we had been developing, so they invited me to join the two of them on a private trip to meet with various leaders around the country. I was excited about this trip and the possibilities God was setting up, but it was also a harder venture to go out on as our newest daughter, Aliyah, had just been born a few days before I was leaving. Interestingly enough, "Aliyah," is a Hebrew word that means to ascend or to return, specifically in regard to Jews returning to Zion.

While there, I also reconnected with the woman from the U.K. we had been introduced to. I started to share with her that Destiny, our family and I all felt led to come stay in Israel for a longer season sometime soon, potentially even that next year. She said they were looking for a family like us to perhaps take over and stay in their ministry house, but I wasn't sure at the time because the house was just outside Bethlehem, in the West Bank. We wanted to love and empower the Palestinian people on behalf of Jesus, and on behalf of Israel, and we had a specific message that pertains to them spiritually but we were unsure if that was the location we should bring our family into for a longer stay.

God dropped another big breadcrumb though while I was traveling with this couple. They took me to meet and stay overnight with a couple they knew on the coast, he was a concert pianist from Russia, and she was from the U.S. and among other things ran a natural health business of sorts, something our family has long been ingrained with. I really enjoyed meeting this couple, certainly one of the highlights of the trip. I shared much of our story and how it related to Israel, and what we still felt was to come. He paused at the end of my sharing in a deliberate way, agreeing with something I said. Then he offered, "That's just it, Israel is waiting for Ruth to come!" And then he played an impromptu, anointed, prophetic song on the piano over me. Both his statement, and the song felt like they were agreeing with and even activating what God had given us about magnifying Ruth chapter 2, when she as a foreigner ventured into Boaz' fields and through such became part of the true "family" redemption.

I returned home to California and after sharing with Destiny and the kids, our call to go and stay in Israel for a longer period only grew. We began to feel that we should prepare to move out of our house and make ourselves "mobile," so that we were ready to go when God said it was time. So, by January, we packed up our home, put much of it in storage, and got on the road planning to stay between a missionary house as well as a couple of homes of family and friends until God made it clear how and when we were supposed to go to Israel.

"Going" to Israel isn't the same as many other nations. The visa process can be very challenging; costs, vehicles, housing, etc. were extra-large obstacles that many of our friends and contacts over there had warned us of. We needed God to show up and make things clear. But for now, it was about saying yes and making ourselves available.

Just as we started to get on the road, God began to open doors and bring quick confirmations. We heard back again from our friend, Mary Jane, the British woman in Israel who had offered her ministry house for us to come and take over for a time. We had somewhat dismissed it before because of location, but now, suddenly, God clued us in on something else about that location that might change our minds.

"Remember," Mary Jane reminded us, "The house you would be in is actually right there amid the very fields of Ruth and Boaz."

We could hardly believe it. God had given us such a clear message about Ruth chapter 2, had continued to speak to us, and through us about it. We felt the call to Israel, stepped out without knowing how or where we would land, and now we're being offered a home right on those very fields of Ruth and Boaz.

Still, we continued to pray as we drove for further confirmation—and peace—in our spirits. As we traveled, that peace started to grow, we were pretty sure this was a door we were supposed to walk through. We pulled up to In "n" Out Burger to get lunch for the kids at a location we stopped at often on that route. We pulled through the drive-thru thru and at the first window, a young man waited to take payment. For some reason, I looked at his nametag, his name was Israel. I laughed and thought, "Well that's funny, and coincidental." We then pulled up to the second window, where a young lady waited with our food. On her nametag it read, "Galilee," our daughter's name, one of our favorite places in Israel, and a name we rarely if ever, heard or saw in the States.

Those might seem like small things, but they were some of those "signs that make you wonder." We continued to cement our yes before the Lord and started to plan to leave in March. As we got back on the highway, there was the most beautiful rainbow, we had ever seen right over us. It was one of those God moments where He was showing up all around us and bringing His words to life that He had spoken to us years before.

14 - To Israel

a gold country treasure hunt: part 1

chapter 15
a gold country treasure hunt: part 1

When we came back from our few-month stint in Israel based on the fields of Ruth and Boaz, we felt the Lord leading us to contend for parts of California while also expanding on the "family of God" message that is so foundational in the Boaz and Ruth story. But there was a series of connections that only God could set up to lead to such, a breadcrumb trail led by His voice if you will. This one is quite the winding path, but full of God encounters and God's amazing faithfulness on display.

Rewind a little back to our first trip to Israel, we had visited a very special prayer house in Jerusalem. As we were seeking the Lord that day, God highlighted a man sitting by us in the back. He was wearing a hat from the San Francisco Giants baseball team, but more than that, there was something very familiar in my spirit. I was sure I knew him from somewhere, I just didn't know where. So, before we left, I went up to introduce myself to him and asked where he was from. His name was Jim, his wife, Becky, and it turned out he was not only from California, but he was from the very town I had grown up in, Fresno, which is where we were basing for the time in between our stints in Redding and Israel. Neither of us could believe that we had to come to the back row of a prayer house in Jerusalem just to meet someone else from Fresno. But that's how God works sometimes. We exchanged contact information and hoped to connect sometime when back in the States.

Once we were around the Fresno area again (at least in and out), I reached out to Jim to see if there was a time we could hook up and get to know one another a little better. We set up a time to come over to their place for dinner and find out how or why our crazy Fresno/Jerusalem connection was coming together. His wife, Becky, answered the door, hugged us with open arms and said, "You are Bill and Julie's kids!" Indeed, Bill and Julie are my parents, but I had no idea how she knew them. I soon discovered that my parents used to be her youth leaders back when she was in Junior High. What a small world! And it took a prayer house in Jerusalem to figure this out.

We had an amazing time catching up, getting to know one another, and visiting that night. The more we talked about the Lord, Israel, and other visions and missions the Lord had put before us, the more they were convinced we had to meet another like-hearted pioneer friend of theirs named Josh. It was already almost 10 pm, but they called Josh anyway and he zipped right over. We probably could've talked and prayed all night, but we covered what we could within a couple of hours. Josh had some similar veins of calling as us, specifically pertaining to California, Israel, John 17, and rebuilding the family of God according to Who He intended us to be.

Now, fast forwarding back to us returning to Central CA from Israel, and it felt like Josh and I had somewhat of a mission to pioneer and uncover together in the region. He and I were at a lunch meeting talking about the area, specifically the California Gold Country, often referred to as the Motherlode, when I suddenly heard this still, small voice in my spirit saying, *"I'll show it to you. The map of the 'Motherlode' looks a lot like the map of Israel."* I didn't say anything in the meeting, as it sounded a little far-fetched to me, even odd. But when I went to do a search, I almost couldn't believe it. The shape of the two areas was incredibly similar, and at that point, I knew this was the region we were supposed to contend for during this season, while we continued to build the message about re-building God's house. And Josh ended up being a very key part and connector for us to be able to take ground by faith in that area.

So, there were two things really going on that we were pioneering and contending for. One was how and where to get positioned in California's gold country. We didn't know anyone there personally, but Josh knew some family friends who had a big, empty house they were selling right in the middle of gold country. This set us up to take our first vision trip into the area and ask the Lord how to move forward.

The second primary thing we had going on was to elaborate on some of the messages God had given us about rebuilding His house/family. That very much included the Boaz and Ruth story, a message about "God's family structure" that is somewhat of a life message for us, and a concept God had given me those couple years before called, "If God Had A House..."

After vision tripping into gold country, it was time for Destiny, the kids and I to venture back up to stay at the missionary house in Redding for a month or two. The place was cared for by an older couple who were former missionaries themselves, and the home was an incredible blessing and provision for us as we remained "mobile" in this pioneering season. We have many good memories there, but few match up to what happened shortly after we arrived in February of 2017.

I was just starting to write a new book, _If God Had A House._ The book was going to be somewhat of a prophetic, almost allegorical experience based on the premise of; If God had a house in your neighborhood, what would it be like? The point of the book was/is to bring to life and help spur the rebuilding of the "family structure" aspect of God's house. It aligned with part of our focus in Israel as well, as we see Israel as the epicenter of God's family. Thus, it was a key place to begin the "mission" of rebuilding His house according to family.

More than the book itself, I will never forget the encounter/dream I had while staying there during that season. It was early morning, around 5 am, and I was somewhere between asleep and awake praying. Suddenly I heard a knock at the door. Surprised, I jumped out of bed and went to see who was there. I opened the door and there was what looked to be a short, middle-aged Italian man with ashy hair and warm eyes.

"Hi, my name is Angelo. I'm your angel, and I have been waiting for this day. It's one of the most exciting days of my life. I have something for you."

Angelo reached out and handed me a small, lavender ring box that had a tidy, white ribbon wrapped around it. Even in that moment I was flummoxed, in a good way. What could he be giving me? I untied the ribbon carefully, opened the lid, and under the small layers of white tissue paper there was a single, silver house key. And then, he was gone.

a gold country treasure hunt: part 2

chapter 16
a gold country treasure hunt: part 2

At first, I didn't know what to do about my encounter with Angelo, let alone the key. It felt very real—very significant. So, one of the first things I did was to go and buy a small, lavender key ring to put on our current set of keys to remind me of what God had sent us through Angelo.

But what was this for? Was it for an actual house? Did it have to do with the book I was writing? Was it a prophetic key for rebuilding "God's house" according to His family structure? I believe, to an extent, it was a key to open the door to each of those things. So, I continued to work on writing the first part of the book, and we started asking the Lord when and how we were supposed to step towards the gold country region again. We did take a couple of smaller day trips into the region to pray and seek the Lord, but we still believed God had even more of a season planned for us there.

We didn't see any specific doors or places opening in gold country, though we did knock on the door to the house that our friend, Josh's family friend was selling. But we could tell that wasn't where God's long-term grace was at. Once we got into the middle of March, we were reminded of the passage God had given us before some of our other big faith steps; about stepping into the Jordan before it is parted, as that was their way to finally move into their promises. It felt like this was one of those times. So, we waited on the Lord for timing and set a date for late March that we would leave the missions house no matter what, regardless of whether we had a place lined up yet.

It's in those moments when a step like that is approaching that you really start to feel it. It's those moments where you keep yourself from overthinking and stay single-minded rather than double-minded. It is in those moments that, like walking on water, you can't weigh the what ifs of the sea under you or the wind and waves around you, you just keep your eyes on Jesus and continue to step towards the word He gave you.

We let the owners of the missions house know our plans, understanding that we could be back again soon, but we knew we had to get our feet into the land God was calling us to. So, on March 27th, the date the Lord had given us, we started to drive south towards gold country, not knowing yet where we would land. It wasn't until during that drive, our friend Josh happened to reach out and ask where we were and what we were up to. We shared what God had given us and let him know we were already on the way down. Immediately, he brought up a friend of his that he had mentioned to me once before, someone who lived at the southern tip of gold country that had a ministry and a property that really resonated with the message of our new book and mission, and the word we had just released on Elijah List ten days before. He sent our most recent word to these friends, Shaun and Michele, to see if they were around and if they happened to have anyone staying in their guest house, as they often had big groups of visitors or other companies visiting. We were about halfway down when we got a call back from Josh that not only was their guesthouse open, but they loved the word and our message, and would be happy to have us come stay with them.

We really connected well with Shaun and Michele, as well as their vision and hearts for ministry. "Family" was so important to them and how they used their property to love and empower the Body of Christ to be who God created them to be. They loved well and consistently hosted gatherings on their property (and in their home), and even set up a specific gathering for us to share at while we were in the area.

At the same time, we were starting to ask the Lord how He wanted to use this open door. We didn't know this area, nor this family, as of the morning we started driving. And now we already saw God forming something. We started to share with them about our desire to live in the area for a time, but also, like all the others faith ventures and moves, didn't know how we would afford a home or qualify for one. But they were willing to pray and believe with us, and they had the next two to three weeks open in their guesthouse that we were welcome to stay. Praise God!

We started praying through and looking around the area to see if God would highlight any houses, people, or any specific ways the Lord was leading us to move forward. We knocked on a couple of doors (but didn't push, lol) though none of them opened. But Shaun and Michele did mention their older neighbor next door. Her husband had passed away and what was their dream home was now too much for her at her older age. She was fully moved out and looking to sell. It was a big home on six acres and, unfortunately, there was absolutely no way we could afford it. We did set up a showing and meeting with her, both to see the house and just to introduce ourselves, how God had brought us down to Shaun and Michele's, and how we were looking to partner with them, and why being next door would be ideal. We asked about owner financing, renting, you name it, but she was pretty set that she just needed to sell it and be done with it once and for all.

A couple of weeks later, before we left to head back to see some family in Fresno for most of April and May, we checked in with her one more time to see if anything had changed on her end. She assured us that she had no wiggle room, and our only option was if we could buy it from her outright. At least we knew that we had knocked on the door, and perhaps even planted some seeds. In the meantime, despite the "no," we felt we were still supposed to plant here in the gold country region and needed to keep stepping by faith. So, at the end of April, we went back up to Redding, God provided to rent a moving truck, and we emptied our storage unit and moved to a new storage unit down in the Coarsegold area. It might seem like a small thing, but it felt like a prophetic act of faith to start to move our household down there to live.

For June and July, we felt like we had a couple of specific, temporary assignments to finish in Redding while we waited for God to open a door. We stayed at the mission house for the month of June, and then, just when it was going to be full with other guests for the rest of the summer, God provided through one of our projects up there just enough to rent a house for the month of July—a house that just so happened to be on the very street where we used to live before we went to Israel.

The other assignment we felt from the Lord was to finish the book I had been writing, _If God Had A House_. There were a couple connects in the area who had some of the specific expertise we needed, and we felt being in one place without moving around for the month would help dial in the focus needed.

The month went well, I was almost done with the writing and publishing process of the book, and we were approaching the last week of July. We had the option of renting the house for one more month, or, well, we were still believing God for the house in Coarsegold next door to Shaun and Michele. So, I decided one last time I would call Carol, the owner of the home and ask if there was any way we could find a creative way to rent the home. However, this time we were refuted even stronger than before, and in no uncertain terms.

I walked into our room and my Bible was open on the shelf. I wasn't planning to stop as I walked by but as I passed, there was a verse that seemed to jump off the page and grab my attention, drawing me back to the word. ***"Pick up your bed and go to your house,"*** it read. That may seem small, and I understand the context of that verse, but at that moment, it felt very clear what the Lord was saying to us. We believed we were supposed to be living in that house. We believed by faith that it was ours, at least for that season. And if we truly believed that then we needed to take God at His word. So, we let the landlord of that current, monthly rental know that we would be leaving at the end of July as planned. We felt God said to pick up what we had and go to our house. Thus, we put everything in motion to leave in just a few days at the end of the month.

I finished everything with the book, got the last endorsement back and felt a release in my spirit like we had accomplished what we were supposed to while there. We would be leaving in just three days and trust that God would make a way between now and then. Just after I closed my computer, my phone rang. It was Carol from the house in Coarsegold.

"Joey, I don't know why I'm even doing this. But I guess if you can get the money together by the end of the month, I need three months of rent to cover my bills and deposit. Then we can make this work."

Destiny and the kids were out on a walk, but I didn't hesitate. "Yes," I said. "We can do that. We'll see you in a couple of days!"

We left on the very day we had already planned and put in motion once the Lord gave us that word to pick up our bed and go to our house, and by the time we reached Coarsegold God had provided enough for the full three months we needed to give her to sign the contract for the house. God did it again! We were amazed, you'd think we wouldn't be at this point, but as faithful as He is it's still a fresh feeling each time we get to join the Lord out of the boat and on the water.

We had an amazing season in gold country where God did a lot, in our family, in the area, more trips to Israel, and great connections that helped to keep moving forward and building the kingdom. And, most of all, we got to partner with the Living God once again.

growing
family

chapter 17
growing family

After a fruitful season in Coarsegold, CA, we felt led by the Lord to move back up north to a small town in the mountains north of Redding. Some close friends and ministry partners — the Duttons — were living there, and there was an opportunity to take some of the identity and empowerment resources we had developed and work on putting them to use in a public high school setting.

The principal welcomed us — and our training — with open arms and hired us as somewhat of a part-time contractor to partner with some of the teachers and classes and put our material to use as a part of building the culture of the school. Likewise, the athletic director, Todd Carson, adopted our core values and plan as a foundational culture for the entire athletic program, though we primarily worked with the two varsity basketball teams.

We won't go too much into what that season entailed mission-wise, or into the multiple miracles that were also needed to make that move and end up living in a 14,000 square foot,100+ year-old dance hall that we converted into a town youth center. What we really want to share is how God continued to expand our family — despite our unique journey — and it was during this season that a major one of those testimonies came to fruition.

Back in 2009, after Galilee was born and our adoptions of both Anna (Kelemua) and Ayni were complete, it seemed like our family of six might be large enough — certainly bigger than we had originally expected. Wow, were we wrong! (Thankfully!) Because of how wrong we were, I scheduled an appointment for a vasectomy assuming it was the right thing to do. I went through the first pre-appointment, and everything was fine and as planned. But it was after that appointment, before the real deal, that I believe I heard the most important word I've ever received from the Lord, *"You're not done yet."*

"What?" I thought to myself. We had four amazing daughters, we lived unconventional lives (to say the least), and we thought our family was complete. But it was such a clear word from the Lord, and Destiny was fully supportive of canceling and trusting God for more kids if that's what He wanted, so I called off the procedure and we went about our lives. However, somewhat surprisingly, no pregnancies came during those next four years.

It wasn't until we were moved back to Colorado that Destiny started having a few unique health scares. It turned out that they were caused by some of the changes in her levels from being pregnant! God navigated us through what she needed to restore some of her levels and be healthy, and we soon found out we were having our first baby boy!

I am Joseph William LeTourneau the 4th, which is somewhat rare these days to see a family line like that go into that many generations. This was exciting for our whole family realizing that we were going to have a boy who would be the 5th. Destiny found a group of midwives and prepared to have the baby as naturally as possible. But once labor came around, there were some difficulties. It was a long and tough labor, though it progressed pretty far along until our little guy was stuck, his forehead was pressed up against her and the cord was wrapped around his neck, not to mention Destiny was in a lot of pain. Despite the natural births with our other girls, we were suddenly being taken in for an emergency C-section, for her sake and our son's. Thankfully, all was well and Joseph William LeTourneau V, who we call William, was our 5th child, born 5 years to the day after Galilee, on the 5th floor, at 5 am. The number 5 means grace, and we knew this pregnancy, Des' health, and our son's birth, and life, were marked by God's grace.

Our daughter, Aliyah, came a little more than two years later. After a C-section, most hospitals won't allow you to have a natural birth. But we had great midwives and Destiny learned and persevered through the obstacles of such and had Aliyah at our home in Redding just a few months before we had gotten on the road and spent that extended stay in Israel on the fields of Boaz and Ruth.

It was during a later stint in Israel that, two years later, we found out Destiny was pregnant again. But upon arriving home in the States, she went through a tough miscarriage (as if there are any other kind), and that baby went straight to heaven.

We still didn't know if we were "done" yet, or should I say if God was done expanding our family. Destiny, and I, as much as we can have our own thoughts or feelings about the matter in certain seasons, thinking our family might be complete, always want God to know He has our yes. And once you meet these precious one's you can't ever imagine your life or family without them! We weren't "trying" per se, but we were open and leaving it in God's hands. And, during a time in the world, especially in western countries, when growing families and birthrates are dropping more and more, we know how much God values family, and children.

"Behold, children are a heritage from the Lord, the fruit of the womb is a reward. Like arrows in the hand of a warrior, so are the children of one's youth. Happy is the man who has his quiver full of them..." (Psalm 127:3-4)

But I'll never forget April 8, 2019 once we were in McCloud, that mountain town north of Redding. We were living in that humongous dance hall and I was sitting with the Lord in our living room in the apartment upstairs. I wasn't in a fervent time of prayer, more just sitting with the Lord and abiding in Him. That's when I unexpectedly heard that still small voice again. *"You're such a good dad and mom, so I'm entrusting you with more. But not at the expense of your family."*

To be honest, at the moment, I wasn't even thinking about more children so I misinterpreted what God was saying. I thought maybe the Lord was saying that because we were stewarding our family before Him, He was about to expand our purpose and calling into "more," but that it wouldn't be in a way that made our family suffer. It felt like a strong, encouraging, almost pointed moment with the Lord. It wasn't until a few weeks later that we found out Destiny was actually pregnant! And then that word from the Lord made far more sense, especially once we had gone over the calendar, mixed with ultrasound, and found out that the baby was likely conceived on April 7th or 8th, right when the Lord had spoken what He did.

However, laws in California had continued to change, and now most midwives with a full practice couldn't aid in births for someone who was having what they call a "V-back," a natural birth after a C-section. Even though Destiny had already given birth naturally since her C-section, it didn't matter to the laws that were put in place. We really prayed about how to handle this birth. Destiny didn't want to have her in a hospital, she again wanted to have the baby at home. And it had long been a desire of hers to have an unassisted, natural birth at home with just she and I present. I was open to this, as I had been very present and involved in all the births of our children, but I also understood the realities and knew we/I would need a lot of God's supernatural help and grace. A lot!

Thankfully, Destiny's pregnancy went very smoothly again this time. She spent hours upon hours, day after day researching, preparing, planning, all that she could do to be well prepared for an at-home, unassisted birth. I listened to what she needed to prepare me with, but mostly, my preparation was really before the Lord. I needed to let God prepare my spirit so that I would approach birth and delivery with God's peace and trust His grace to perfect my weaknesses in the situation. But Destiny was peaceful and confident about it, and we both felt a peace from the Lord about going this route, even though it felt like a huge step of faith.

My confidence and peace were boosted one night a couple of weeks before our new little girl would be born. I was walking through our house, praying, and there in the living room, up against the wall right in between the doors to our bedroom and the bathroom, I saw what I perceived to be an angel. The angel was dressed differently than some, or even I might expect. She almost looked like what we typically think Jesus' mother, Mary, wore in many of the scenes around Jesus' birth. However, I wasn't exactly sure why. So, I thought I would just ask the Lord.

"Why is there an angel right here specifically, and why is she dressed in this unique way?" I inquired of the Lord.

I felt the Lord remind me that I had been praying for His angels to be present with us, and specifically with this birth and delivery coming up. I know how much God uses angels in our lives as servants that help protect, minister and bring about His will (and so much more!). We realize that we need His heavenly hosts as our "team" if we are going to accomplish the kingdom building that we're supposed to in this time in the world. And again, I had prayed for angels specifically to be there to help with the birth since it was just going to be Destiny and myself. It's just that I didn't expect to see the answer in this pronounced of a way. Though I was thankful that I did.

What I sensed back from the Lord after I asked, was that the unique clothes I saw on the angel were specific to its role at that time for us. The clothing resembled "Mary" because Mary was/is a picture of supernatural childbirth. And this angel was here with us in response to our prayers to help with Destiny's labor and delivery, and our daughter's birth.

Two weeks later, Destiny went into labor, not in the bathroom, but right there five feet from the spot where that angel stood in the living room. She finished labor in the bathroom next to where the angel stood, and that's where I was privileged to catch and deliver our amazing blessing. Labor and delivery for Destiny and the baby was as quick, smooth, and seemingly supernatural as ever. I was in awe as I delivered our little girl, immediately going into utter thanks and praise while declaring God's goodness. Then calling up to the rest of our family, "She's here!"

Our amazing daughter, Hallelujah (Halle) Rose LeTourneau, joined our family in the most simple, smooth, yet supernatural way. With all our crazy steps or ventures of faith, very little could match this moment of what I felt God do for Destiny, for Halle, for me, and for our family. It felt like perhaps the most supernatural moment I had ever been a part of. God had been so present since the moment on April 8th when He announced to me that He was expanding our family, to finding out He really was three weeks later, to see that special angel there with us, to watching God bring to the time of birth, and deliver our amazing daughter. Thanks God!

running

for

congress

chapter 18

running for congress

I know what you're probably thinking. You read that chapter title and thought, *"after reading about your lives, in what world are you qualified to run for Congress?"* Don't worry, I thought — *and felt* — the same thing many times. In most typical ways, I wouldn't be qualified to run for that kind of political office. But we didn't run a very typical race, either. For years, I sensed something of a "governmental call" from the Lord. I never knew if it would be literal or more spiritually speaking. I've had specific words and encouragements spoken into my life and family from the Lord, and people, and I have always felt a draw or connection to those like Joseph, Daniel, Zerubbabel and the like. I can't say that I had specifically planned on running for Congress. But one day early that fall, all the dots started to connect, and we believed we were supposed to run, and run not so much for an office as much as with a message that would impact culture.

We didn't want to be in power, we wanted to serve and empower others. We wanted to take power back from politics again and give it to people so that they could have the freedom and courage to live out a government of true hope and purpose. And yet, the step into this unknown political world of government would require a new level of courage for myself and my family as well.

At the beginning, I would wake up and it would feel very foreign, like I was David wearing Saul's armor. This was always a great reminder not to put on the world's expectations for what our campaign should look like, but to feel free to be authentic and to engage in this battle according to whom God has made us to be, not who that part of the world requires you to be. My favorite part of the campaign was the daily dependence on God and running this race with Him. I had to receive our marching order, when to step and when to stop, from Him. I couldn't react to the world's expectations or pressures or else that would give power back to the political and the typical.

How I ran mattered much more to us than whether we would win. I could not see the government we hoped for come alive if we subscribed to the usual process, as we cannot do the same things over and over while yet expecting a different result. The only way to see change would be to change the way we went about our day-to-day campaign, regardless of what that meant. And sometimes, it was very uncomfortable. Most of the time, it was incredibly rewarding and such an intimate process with God. I had to consistently come face to face with the question that decides where our hope is anchored: *Where am I putting my trust?*

There was so much involved in registering to run and even getting on the ballot. From the paperwork, the deadlines, the signatures and all the conversations while gathering those signatures. And then there was articulating where we stood on so many different issues in interviews, debates, etc. Yet, for us, our goal was to show a new way forward, not just add more weight to one side.

Though we both come from conservative values, we ran for office to be prophetic, not political. We wanted to take government back from politics again, so we ran as "Independent" or "No Party Preference" because it was most authentic to our voice. We ran for reformation, to put people before politics again, to go beyond the issues that divide us, and to point the way forward while healing the roots of our culture. Though we weren't successful in winning our election, the morning after, I still felt so much victory because something new had been born. The election or position wasn't the baby or promise being born. Rather, our campaign, for us, was the process of labor and delivery to help bring a new, yet ancient and necessary government to life for the time we are now living in.

From that season and all that was developed, we wrote and released a new book called, *Government of Hope: Blueprint for Reformation*. It's about the increase of Jesus' kingdom government that was prophesied about in Isaiah 9:6-7. It is built around strategic blueprints of how we as people can create lasting, grassroots change in and through our communities. It's about us being the government that God created us, the Ekklesia, to be. We don't have to have a political seat to usher in true government, and that's a big part of what our nation — and the world — needs most right now. They need to be *shown* something different.

After we wrote this book, it was clear that God was preparing us to leave California and had a different harvest field and homebase ahead. At the time, it was right smack in the middle of Covid, the lockdowns, policy changes and the information wars that came with it. We felt the invitation to break out of the lockdowns and drive community to community to share with people how to empower a true government of hope right where they are.

So, at a time when most people were locked down, we prayed and sought the Lord about what turned into a twenty-state trip around the country with two primary goals: empower communities on how to mobilize with fresh, kingdom blueprints, and find the next home base and community God was leading us to build in and from.

our 20-state journey

chapter 19
our 20-state journey

Before we began this twenty-state journey God gave us a few directives and a couple of specific promises. One of these promises was based around the premise of stepping into a part of our "inheritance." When I say inheritance, I'm not just talking about the financial type of inheritance that is passed on within a family, rather, I'm speaking of the spiritual heritage that was established and set in motion by previous generations.

Earlier in the book I mentioned a little about my great, great uncle, R.G. LeTourneau. He was famously known as "God's Businessman," as he was an inventor and innovator who built huge earth moving equipment, offshore oil rigs, helped build needed equipment for the war, and gave a lot into missions as well as churches and discipleship camps here in the U.S. Besides the inventions, as we shared in an earlier chapter, R.G and his wife were perhaps most known for living out the "reverse tithe" as some would call it, giving 90% and living off 10%. R.G., his wife, and their family were known for their big, pioneering faith on all these fronts — and more — and laid a legacy for our family that is an honor to come from. For us, that's a huge inheritance!

I have never been the engineer that he was, but pioneering big and new endeavors by faith is something that has been a predominant theme in my life and our family. Even with such, we felt God was saying that there was more to step into from our inheritance — especially connected to R.G.— that would continue to be part of our calling moving forward.

As we prepared to step out, Destiny received a word, "Adventure Awaits." And then for the next however many weeks not only did we see that word come alive, but we continued to bump into different versions of that phrase wherever we went. But even more importantly, there was a word from Jeremiah that God had given us years before that He re-highlighted before this trip, especially to Destiny.

"Do you seek great things for yourself? Do not seek them; for behold I will bring adversity on all flesh,' says the Lord. But I will give your life to you as a prize in all places, wherever you go." (Jeremiah 45:5)

That's something we always try to keep at our plumbline as we walk with the Lord, but especially as we set out on this journey. It was important that we kept all hopes, vision and expectation in His hands and gave Him room to surprise us with His best answers, that are so much better than ours. When we allow Him to, He truly does give us our lives as a prize in all places, wherever we go!

In the weeks leading up to getting on the road, we started to reach out to a few people in different communities, and one connection led to another to the point where we had a baseline of stops to meet with people, speak, and share about kingdom community strategies. We packed up our home, put most of it in storage, and filled our suburban with what we might need for the next couple of months or for when we found the home we were supposed to base out of next. From the start, it was like many of our trips, and our moves, where we only had the funds to get started, and then would trust God to provide as we moved forward with Him.

Our first stop was back in the Denver area for a couple of days, reconnecting with family and friends. We didn't have the funds yet to get to our second stop in Amarillo, Texas, but just as we started to leave Denver on schedule, going out the door that morning, God provided just enough to make the trip. Then, we had some very fruitful visits with different friends in Amarillo, talking about what God was doing down there and reconnecting with some who we had done ministry there with years before. After a few days, we were on our way to Fort Worth, Texas for the rest of the week. Some good friends hosted us at their Friday night Shabbat homegroup, and we found the people and place to be very open and ripe to the message and blueprints God had us carry. We followed up with some more meetings that week, and one person in particular, a new friend named Jason, encouraged us to add Cody, Wyoming somewhere on this journey. He had lived with an amazing family and community in Cody who had mentored him and had been a great support. He thought the blueprints we were sharing would fit well with what God had called them to. As usual, I told Jason we'd be very open to adding Cody as a stop when we circle back to the west if God opened the door, and that we should stay in touch. But while there, the Fort Worth area really resonated for us with what we felt God doing and the community that was there.

Next, we headed back up to Amarillo for another couple of nights, mostly to pick up our daughter Galilee who had stayed behind that week to learn and help with horses on a ranch. Then we were headed up to Oklahoma for a couple of days with a family we had never met, but who had been doing some awesome things in the community to build the kingdom and loving and empowering others well. This stop was less about looking into that area and more about connecting partnership-wise with this family and their vision. Thankfully, by the time we were supposed to get on our way towards Nashville, God provided enough funds to make the trip and to pay for our upcoming Air Bnb.

Nashville was mostly about meeting up with another family who had a similar vision for empowering community hubs around the States, and Internationally. For an extended period of time, they had lived missionary, moving around while living in a converted school bus. We were looking at ways we may be able to partner, and they were on the road visiting various communities as well. It was powerful waiting on God together, discussing future endeavors, but also, the next stop for each of us was still forming. There were a couple of directions we could go next and still hit some of our planned stops on time, same with them, but we all really wanted God's order for what He was trying to accomplish.

Just before we were to leave God gave both our families clear direction, but different directions. We wouldn't be going to the next community together. God was calling them east towards North Carolina and the Lord took us up north to Michigan. As we drove through Ohio and into Michigan we got a call from our new friend, Jason, from our time in Fort Worth. Apparently, he had given out a copy of our book, Government of Hope, and the person he gave it to recognized our last name. He asked Jason if we were related to R.G. LeTourneau. We hadn't discussed this while in Texas, so Jason had no idea, hence his call. I told him yes, that R.G. is a distant uncle whose legacy is important to our family. At that point, he was even more amazed:

"Remember," he asked, "the family I mentioned from Cody, WY, who I thought would connect with your family and message? Well, when I stayed with them, they shared a lot with me about someone that sounds like R.G. LeTourneau and gave out dozens of his books. They have an earth moving and excavation business among other things, let me call Jim to find out if it's the same person they taught me about all those years."

I was certain it was, as was he by this point. And sure enough, Jason called back a little while later once we were in Grand Rapids to let us know he had talked to Jim & Sarah Nicholson, and sure enough, R.G.'s book was the one they had given out so frequently, and his testimony was a big inspiration to their family, their business and mission. That's one of those times you have a good "God-laugh." And now, Jason was even more determined for Cody to be one of our stops. He planned to check with Jim again and see if they would want us to stop through.

In Michigan, we had two sets of other close friends, both of whom we had worked with or ministered with in the past, in two different cities — Grand Rapids and Detroit. Both became great stops! In fact, our partnership and work with these families — the Wielhouwers and Henrion's — has only increased since that time, and in very fruitful ways all over the world. Also, it would be on our way to our next stop in Ohio where we were scheduled to stay between one to two weeks. Besides planning for the future with them, we used the time to seek the Lord for where He was taking us later in the trip after Ohio. We had a couple of dates we left unplanned on purpose, specifically Rosh Hashanah, the Jewish New Year (September 18-20th that year), feeling there was something strategic to where we would be over that weekend. It was one of those situations where we wanted to make plans, but it felt like we needed to keep our faith and patience working together and trust God to show up. At the same time, our daughter, Mercy, was in California getting ready to start her Senior year at a new school, largely for basketball's sake. Since the beginning of the trip, we were planning to fly her out once we found the place God was leading us to as a new family base. Our older girls, Anna & Ayni, were both in California still, too.

We moved on to our trip and meetings in Ohio, meeting an amazing new family, the Littleton's, and having some great meetings and community discussions while we were there. We still didn't have confirmation of where to go next, specifically for that Rosh Hashanah weekend. And on top of that, we needed to know where to book Mercy a ticket to meet up with us soon. I finally got some clarity in prayer, the Lord giving me a date, September 16th, and directing me to have Mercy fly into Denver on that day. He would show us where He was taking us from there.

Towards the end of our stay in Ohio, we got a call again from Jason in Texas. He had talked to Jim and Sarah Nicholson again, and they would love to have us come out and connect with them and the community in Cody. But there was only one catch, they had a busy schedule on the horizon, and it would have to be the weekend of September 18-20, which clearly were the exact dates God had us keep open, waiting to see how He would fill it. So, we let them know that those dates were perfect, and even that God had us reserve them ahead of time for something special. Not only that but driving through Denver to pick up Mercy at the airport on September 16 would fit perfectly before a drive up into northwestern Wyoming. God had ordered it all perfectly ahead of time, we just hadn't gotten to see it until now.

Our spirits really started to feel activated as we made the drive, like God was setting up something special. Our daughter Anna had just recently been married to Neb in California, and though Ayni was out there as well, as we drove towards Cody, WY, God started to really highlight Ayni on my heart. I felt like God was going to have something there for her too, so much so that I started to weep over it, even though I had no idea what it might be. As I shared with Destiny, it was confirming to hear that she was sensing the same thing from the Lord. So, we called Ayni and let her in on a few more details of where we were going, and how God had set it up. She wasn't eager to leave California at the time, and she really knew nothing of Wyoming nor had any natural draw there. None of us did for that sake. Mostly, we just planted the seed that we felt God was doing something there and that she was part of it, whatever that might be.

Once we got to Denver to pick up Mercy, Jim and I talked by phone to get to know each other a little more before we made the trip up. Turns out, not only were they connected to the R.G. story, but a Pastor they knew from Colorado had come up multiple times and had left them with a couple of my books of all things. And since they always wanted to meet a LeTourneau (due to R.G.'s story), after receiving our books, they had prayed that God would bring us through someday — long before Jason ever called them to mention meeting us. Now, you can imagine, we were even more blown away by what God was doing.

We arrived in Cody, spoke at their church the next day, had a wonderful time meeting a variety of people, but mostly spent time with Jim, Sarah and their family. They had four young adult children still living on the property and working with their family earth-moving business, and one daughter who was already married with a family of her own.

We quickly learned how many people, especially missionaries, had come through whom they had housed that summer. And the absolute last thing we wanted to do was be a burden. However, our times visiting about family, mission, stories and forward vision about what we saw God doing, especially in communities such as this, the more we were drawn together. They had a guest home that had just opened up for us to live in, which was such a blessing after being on the road. And a lot of what we did fit their vision with their property, and where they hoped and believed to see things eventually go. We were ready to put down roots again, or at least build a nest and the Nicholson's were quickly becoming like family. After the long faith-trip, God had done what He said, He would in taking us to a new family base. Not only that, but it was a family who had built so much already upon the testimony of our family heritage with R.G. LeTourneau, bringing us to a place to join them in stepping even further into our inheritance and what God wanted to do with such.

After a week, knowing we were going to set up our new home base in Cody, we still had to drive back to Denver for Mercy to fly to California for school. On the way down, our suburban that was now over 200,000 miles, had its engine start to blow out about 3 hours from our hotel. We prayed as we drove, and God helped us just barely roll into our hotel parking lot. From there we got the problem diagnosed and then sent down to some great family friends in Colorado Springs, the Carter's, who own three Napa stores and were willing to help gradually rebuild the engine for us at cost. That was another huge praise!

God provided for a rental suburban, and a few more nights at our hotel in

Denver, and then we packed up to move to Cody for the foreseeable future. Not only that, but someone who had heard us speak about our mission and faith adventures in Cody heard about our Suburban, she had an extra van, and God moved on her heart to donate it to our family. So not only did we have a new home, but God had already provided a wonderful new family vehicle as well.

To top it off, still, a month after arriving in Cody, Ayni finally agreed to fly out and see all God had set up, especially with what we felt for her before even landing in Cody. Unfortunately, she arrived at one of the most intense cold fronts, down to negative twenty degrees. As much as she probably wanted that to stop her from coming, God continued to speak to her heart and a few months later, she moved out to join us in Wyoming. And several months later we now fully understood why we felt so strongly from the Lord about her as we drove to Cody for the first time. She became engaged to the Nicholson's oldest son, David. The Nicholson's already felt like family, but now they truly were! It's always amazing how God turns those little prompts that may seem insignificant into life-changing blessings.

freedom

chapter 20

freedom u

Several months after moving to Cody, WY, while dreaming and praying with the Nicholson family, God started to stir our hearts to a new form of a "re"-newed vision we'd had for years. We had prayed into starting a youth empowerment center in multiple locations, including Ethiopia and Colorado, but it has not come to pass yet.

In one sense, a lot of the training we apply does not require a building. It travels well and is adjustable to people and communities by nature. But as we were landing in Cody, we kept feeling the pull towards setting up a place that was about more than training, but an experience like my book, _If God Had A House_, or a place that could be like a Petrie dish in a way, bringing people and their unique identity and gifting, to mix with the Father's DNA, and then be able to empower them out into their own path of purpose and multiplication. Essentially, it was about making disciples of all nations, that's what _Freedom U_ started as, and our bread and butter was to do so through identity and empowerment. A building would just be a place to cultivate that and make and send disciples from.

Jim showed me a building out on the west side of town, an old church that had sat empty for some years now. It was a large building, and needed a lot of work, but there was something about it that felt full of redemptive possibilities. Jim was acquainted with the owner, who lived between Cody and Arizona, and set up a meeting for the next time he would be in town in early spring. Once that time came around, we prepared a lot of pieces of our vision, how we wanted to operate, and had a great meeting with him. We didn't get a full yes for the building, as he was still trying to sell it, but we asked for the time being if we could use the front lobby area to start our initial local classes in for the first six weeks or so. He graciously allowed us to do so if we took the necessary steps to get that part of the building functional, which wasn't exactly a small thing at the time after sitting empty for so long. Thankfully the Nicholson's had a lot of ability or contacts in those ways to help fix it up and make that area useable.

The classes started off well and helped us build new relationships as well as find those who might want to be involved more long term. As we started to wrap up the six-week course, I felt the Lord nudging us to plan a prayer and worship time at the building to contend for full use of it. We weren't yet allowed in any other part of the building, but I felt the Lord give us a specific date, so we went ahead and started to plan the gathering by faith, even if it meant we had to meet outside to pray and contend from there. Some good momentum started to build and just a week or so before the gathering was to take place, the owner let us know that he was going to give us full access to the whole building — upstairs, downstairs, the sanctuary, etc.— free of charge. We simply had to get utilities hooked up and we would be the ones responsible for caring for what was needed as if it were our own. So, by the time we had the worship and prayer meeting, God had already provided the main worship hall to gather in for that date.

After that, God started providing more and more funds and other resources to fix the place up, to design it, fill it, repair it and build out the vision. It was a huge building with two floors, almost fifteen rooms and offices as well as a giant worship hall that looked like an upside-down wooden ark. And God brought more and more people around us to help make the vision come to life. It was less about large group audiences, and much more about a community of disciples coming together, building something both seen and unseen, as well as being empowered to go out in new ways in their own lives and calling.

During that time, the Wielhouwer family I mentioned from Grand Rapids in the last chapter moved by faith to join us all in Cody. They became an integral part of what God was doing and building with Freedom U. They had a close relationship with a ministry in Uganda, more specifically with a husband-and-wife leadership team, Isaac and Alice, that had just taken on the role of head chaplain at somewhat of a trade school for college-age students in Uganda. Their desires for the students matched much of our vision with Freedom U, as well as a lot of what we had already done in Ethiopia years prior. So, we prepared a team of trainers and media specialists to go with Dede and put together a Freedom U discipleship week there in partnership with the school, as well as film a mini-documentary about finding hope hidden in unlikely places.

They had a powerful trip, and the relationships and partnership only grew from there. Destiny and I joined a second trip out just a few months later, where we also had our friend/family from Ethiopia, Alex and his friend, Dashm, join us to help with some specific practical needs on the campus. Alex was thrilled to now, himself, be a missionary in Uganda. He talked about the privilege of getting to take what God had done with him in Ethiopia, and the movement of discipleship and empowerment that started later, and now helps give the same to the youth in Uganda. Meanwhile, God helped us establish further roots in the community and Alex and his friend Dashm extended their stay for well over a month to continue to help. Meanwhile, our daughter Mercy, and one of the Nicholson's sons, Nate, moved to the area to help facilitate the movement that was growing and to come alongside Isaac and Alice with the young leaders we were discipling at the school. It was awesome watching the relationships they built with those student leaders and the impact they had. And for Destiny and I, it was such a pleasure to send others like them to carry the movement forward and not have it be dependent only on us. That was the picture of empowerment we always hoped to see.

As we came back from that trip, while Mercy and Nate were still in Uganda, after about one year in the building the owner approached us about what the next year would look like. He acknowledged that though he loved what we were doing in the building, and through it to places like Uganda as well, he would need to charge rent for this next year or else find someone else who was ready to rent the space. We weren't too caught off guard by this, and even with something as big or central as a building, we always try and hold loosely before the Lord. We know that God uses buildings, as He had this one. But buildings are only a tool. God's true blueprint is what He is building through His people, His family, and that was the blueprint we moved to Cody with in the first place. That said, we had a big decision to make. The rent was going to go from zero to $3,000 per month, a huge jump. We didn't have those funds yet, but we had watched God provide many more times that amount to fill the building and rebuild it that whole year prior.

As we prayed, we started to remember a word God had given me at the beginning of that year, January of 2022. It is the parable of the wedding feast found in Matthew 22. The call to those putting on the wedding was to go to the highways and byways, much like we had with Ethiopia and other nations in previous years, and what had started and was continuing at that time in Uganda as well. When I had gotten that word earlier in the year, Elijah List sent it out as one of their daily words. I received an e-mail back from a man named Charles in Malawi. He told me that he, and his community were who the word was talking about. And the more I got to know Charles, what God was doing in the area, and the vision he had for the communities there, the more I agreed with him. So, like Uganda, we had a trip coming up to Malawi to do a Freedom U discipleship and empowerment training with over three hundred local community leaders, pastors and emerging young leaders — as well as planned trips into some of their strategic outlying communities.

With all this in mind, as we prayed about the building, and despite all the money we had poured into it, we felt the Lord telling us to give it up. While that might sound like a loss to some, God had started so much there already that was now beginning to multiply out. It wasn't about a potential loss, but about a step forward to take more ground with the Lord. He had already given us the mandate of the highways and bi-ways, and even if we had the $3,000 per month in rent, we realized it would go much further in building out this kind of discipleship and empowerment hubs in Uganda, Malawi, Ethiopia, and beyond. So, just after our Uganda trip, and just before we were scheduled to go lead the training in Malawi, we gave up the building, thanked God for what He had done there, and how He truly had used it as a Petrie dish to bring in DNA, mix it with His, and now, multiply outside of that Petrie dish through other people to other places. It had served its purpose well.

After giving up the building, the closer we got to the Malawi trip, the more we saw God start to grow it into something more. Mercy and Nate planned to fly down from Uganda to meet us and join us for the time in Malawi, and the Nicholson's other son, Daniel, planned to come along as well. They joined Destiny and me, as well as our four younger kids at the time, Galilee, William,

Aliyah and Halle. We loved getting some of our younger kids back involved with some of our international travel, specifically across Africa. After our first four experienced so much, this trip was a grace for them to receive from the Lord, far more than they could have even known.

Once we were going to Malawi, it became natural to stop back in Uganda again since so much was growing there after the first trip. As we continued to pray, we realized that we had a lot of momentum picking back up with Alex in Ethiopia, and we hadn't been back to Addis Ababa in quite a while. So, it became natural to add the Ethiopia stop after Uganda. Then, we figured, "why stop there?" God started to highlight Israel again to us while we were preparing for those three stops across east Africa. We had a lot of former contacts and seeds planted in Israel, but it had felt like a closed door for a few years now ever since COVID 19 had begun. Since things had just opened, we really felt it was the right time to get our feet back on Israel's soil. Each step of the way God continued to provide for the added flights, and different guest house stays. Before we knew it, we had a two-month trip planned between the four nations and watching God take what had started at Freedom U in Cody, lead us to surrender the building part, and now watch as He multiplied it out to the highways and bi-ways faster than we could have imagined. On top of it all, almost the whole Nicholson family decided to meet us in Israel for the last leg of the trip, as it was a trip they had long prayed about and waited for.

I can barely describe the power of what that two-month trip turned into. The people we got to interact with and empower in each nation, the Nicholson's being able to join, and especially for our younger kids getting to experience the Lord through such steps, among such people, in nations such as those. The harvest in Malawi was ripe, and ready. I don't know if I've ever been around such a grassroots community of leaders who were so ready to receive and put their faith into action. It was beautiful! The communities there were set up in a way as we had long prayed for, like Acts 4:31-34. And they were ready to take what they were learning and empower the youth to start growing in the very same. We honestly couldn't have asked for anymore!

In Uganda it was really a continued foundation laying trip. We spent most of our trip this time not doing training but investing in our primary group of leaders and working to identify and empower some emerging young interns to come alongside them. It was a longer stay, but also fruitful for the sake of the long term.

Our trip back to Ethiopia absolutely rocked us. Not only did we get to return to our former home and spend time with Alex and his family, but many of the former street kids we had mentored came around us like family our whole trip. Many had graduated high school with high marks, gone on to college, one was even working in a high-up government position after helping to transform part of the city. And now all they could do was tell us that they wanted to go give others what we had given them all those years. They recognized it was different, that it wasn't just ministry to us, but that it had been about family. They're recognizing that on their own filled our hearts. That's the best way we can describe our time back in Ethiopia, that our hearts were full. And to top it off our younger kids who had never been there also bonded like family with these former street kids, who were now leaders. To watch them protect our kids while we walked the streets, play games with them, or sit around until later hours telling stories of what God had done in their lives, and now Galilee, Will, Aliyah and Halle were getting to hear it firsthand. It was like showing up to a formerly dry field where you had invested every bit of resource, faith and love that you had, only to return years later and find a flourishing, fruitful garden. We were in awe of God!

And Israel, well, Israel would be very different than Ethiopia, Uganda or Malawi, but it turned out to be one of our best trips there ever. Being back in the land for the fall feasts, reconnecting and sharing the vision with leaders we had known previously, experiencing special sites or tastes with the Nicholson, getting to baptize our kids in the Jordan river where Jesus was baptized, and so much more! Most of all, we came back from this two-month trip, finishing with almost three weeks in Israel having God deposit something special and timely for the nation in us once again. Within two weeks of returning, by the end of October, we knew God was calling us to go back to live there for another season. We planned to leave in just two and a half months.

n strategic
& intense
time in
the world

chapter 21
a strategic & intense time in the world

Earlier in our story, when I first discussed our call to Israel, I shared about what God had spoken to me when I was eighteen; that I "would live there in my 30's-40's at a strategic and possibly intense time in the world."

God first started opening the door for our travels to Israel when I was 33, and we had been there for both short and long stays several times thereafter. By this time now I was nearly 42, and things were certainly heating up in the world.

God opened the door for our family to go back to Israel in January of 2023. We would start with the normal three-month visas (visas can be extra difficult in Israel), and stay indefinitely as long as the Lord allowed, or led. But as far as we could see, we would stay for our first three months, then take a trip to Ethiopia for nearly four weeks, and then come back to Israel for another three months as visas allowed.

We were working with and connecting to different leaders from previous stays in the Land, and God had us on several other assignments as well, including partnering with a local, renowned artist who has paintings in both the White House and for Israeli Prime Ministers. For the first three months, we would be moving around the country. Step-by-step, stop-by-stop, we watched God provide for the rental van we needed to fit our family — one big enough to carry a traveling household with us — and for Air BnB's all over the country. We typically stayed anywhere from one week to two weeks at various communities, including multiple stops in Jerusalem, some near Tiberias, a kibbutz just outside of Nazareth, twice in Meggido (more commonly known as the Valley of Armageddon), and on the coast in both Netanya and Zikhron Ya'aqov. Each place had its own purpose, some intended by us and others as led by the Lord and His surprises. We love the culture and the community in Israel, and often feel very much at home.

However, just after arriving, within ten days, things really started to heat up around Israel. Between rockets fired, various scattered terrorist attacks, a lot of turmoil in the West Bank, and large threats from neighboring countries — not to mention what may have been considered the greatest threat, which was the internal turmoil in the political divisions and the mass protests that followed among the people. These weren't just any protests, they were consistent, and some were as large as 200,000 people. It began to cause a lot of division in the nation, both among the people and the government. We knew God had us there at this time to pray and intercede for Israel and God's promises for her. Later in the year, we heard numerous people saying this had been the most intense time in the country in many, many years, coming from multiple enemies as well as internally.

In early spring, when we were getting ready to go to Ethiopia, the protests were intensifying, and threatening to create bigger problems. We were driving from Megiddo to the airport early that morning. As I woke up that day, going through the natural challenge of packing up a big family for an airport run while traveling, I had this sense and picture that we were moving down a very narrow walkway, like a tunnel that was closing in and we were just sneaking through the window on the other side. It was an odd feeling, especially because we weren't hearing anything out of the ordinary about our flights. On top of that, we talked to several close people back in the States that morning on the way to the airport who said we were extra on their hearts, and they were praying.

The traffic was awful that morning. We were considerably late to the airport by typical international travel standards and found ourselves pressed for time once we got there. Beyond those somewhat typical travel circumstances, while nothing was spoken overtly, there was an extra "edge" to most of those we encountered while trying to hurriedly make our flight on time. And despite all the small pushback, thankfully, we made our flight and landed in Ethiopia three and a half hours later. As we were on the tarmac, I turned on my phone and started getting texts asking if we were okay. I had no idea what they were talking about until one of the close friends, who's is also an intercessor, informed me they heard that the international airport in Israel had been shut down. I almost didn't believe it, seeing as we were just there and neither heard nor saw anything that would lead us to believe such. But the more I investigated it, our friend was right. In fact, the airport completely shut down only fifteen to twenty minutes after we took off; we were one of the last planes to leave and apparently, unbeknownst to us, truly had squeezed through a narrow passage and window on our way out.

After another great and fruitful few weeks in Ethiopia, we were very excited to get back to Israel. Things had just started to calm down to a medium intensity and this time, our plan was to try and rent an apartment in Jerusalem as it would be much cheaper than continuous Air BnB's, it would allow us to walk and use public transport instead of the high-cost van, and most of all, we felt it was where the Lord wanted us to be!

Most of that next season was full of a lot of prayer walking, and meetings of still developing work and partnerships. We spent many hours each week out walking as a family, praying over the people and specific locations, as well as putting together videos to help others know how to pray at this strategic and intense time for both Israel, and the world. God opened the door to an amazing apartment, and compared to the process it would take to get approved for most apartments in the city (as we had been told, and even tried), this was as smooth as possible as well as a dream set up and location within Jerusalem. It was a mostly furnished place, and the rental agency just pushed us past any bureaucratic mountains that usually stood in the way.

It was during that season that we also started to pray and contend for further visas. Currently, our visas would expire in July. We wanted to stay much longer, but we knew we couldn't see the big picture and knew God had more going on than we understood. One of those things, we quickly found out, was that Destiny was pregnant again. The pregnancy started out very difficult, and we almost had another miscarriage from the signs. But it was at that point that we really started to pray and declare God's authority, His bloodline, and His promises.

See, we had three miscarriages before among our already growing family. And two of those babies had started in Israel — one just three months before in February. But this time, just three hours after we found out Destiny was pregnant, a longtime family friend and intercessor named La Vonne, wrote us that she had an uncommon but very clear dream the night before, and in the dream, we had eight kids. We hadn't told a single person yet, so this was a special confirmation from God to happen just hours after we found out. Just two days before that, at an international prayer house, a woman looked at Destiny with kind of a twinkle in her eye and said, "you should have more kids." It was not a casual comment either, more like one of those that someone says because they seem to know something but can't share the specifics yet. And then yet another family friend and prayer warrior wrote us within a couple of days, telling us she also had a dream that Destiny was pregnant, and that we had a new baby girl named Abundance.

After all these confirmations and words from people who had no idea, it gave us a lot of faith to pray from when Destiny started to have signs of a potential miscarriage. One night she started spotting heavily and having some discomfort and pain, and I just remember thinking over those different dreams and words from prayer warriors and saying, "No, we are not losing this child. God said we had eight kids. We put the blood of Jesus around us all and decree those promises of life, and life more abundantly." Destiny soon went to a nearby clinic in Jerusalem for a check-up and ultrasound and thankfully all was very good for both Des and our baby. We found out the baby was indeed a "she," and that she was whole and in great health. Thank You Jesus!!

While we were praying and contending for visas and timing as a family, we received a letter from our artist friend in Jerusalem asking on our behalf for a letter to extend our visas. After several visits to the visa department, and one visit that didn't go so well — more of an interrogation treating us as pests — we were at least given a three-month extension that would take us into October. Destiny could only travel up until November, so we needed the Lord's clarity on whether we were supposed to fight to stay, trust for a visa and have the baby in Israel, or if we were supposed to go back to the States to have her there. We prayed, and knocked on several doors, but nothing was quite clear yet. Until one day in late July, just after finishing what could have been a very strategic meeting partnership-wise, I felt a sudden release from the Lord that had not been there when we prayed in weeks prior. Destiny felt the same. Not only that, but we started to feel from the Lord very strongly that we were to leave Israel by mid-September before the fall feasts began. That was somewhat hard as we love the feasts, and especially love being there for them in Israel. However, obedience and alignment with the Lord were and are much more important.

That left a few more questions though. Would we just be back in the States briefly and then returned to Jerusalem after the baby was born? Should we keep our apartment for that option? Or were we to let go of our apartment and move fully back to the U.S. again? That last option wasn't our most preferred personally, as we were feeling more and more at home there. But it became clear that it was the right option.

We arrived back in the U.S. in early September, a little ahead of our timeline from the Lord. And just a few weeks later, that's when the unbelievable tragedy struck Israel on October 7th with the attack from Hamas and the ensuing war on multiple sides. We were thankful God had brought us back when He did, but also, our hearts were with the people and the Land we love so much. We were glued to our phones to hear non-media updates from those we knew on the ground. We could pray, and God knows He would have had our yes to stay through such conflict to keep praying, loving and supporting however we could. At the same time, we were very thankful we weren't caught in the middle of the war having to find a way to evacuate when so many flights were shutting down, or having our kids listen to so many missiles being shot or exploding overhead, as many of our friends and their families there were going through.

Truly, God had demonstrated His word once again in what He had said to me when I was 18. We were indeed living there for one of the more strategic and intense seasons in Israel's recent history, and we got to pray and intercede on behalf of the people and the nation before the far worse atrocities took place. It certainly gave us even a little more of a picture of what the Jewish people go through on a day-to-day basis, and how to pray for that epicenter of God's family and kingdom for the times ahead.

birthing
abundance

chapter 22
birthing abundance

Just as our friend had seen in her dream, we decided we were going to name our new daughter whom Destiny was pregnant with, Abundance. We would call her Adi for short, which means "Gift" in Hebrew.

Not only was Destiny pregnant with Abundance, but ironically God currently also had us in a season contending for abundance for many other places and people as well. We were now more formally partnering with a longtime best friend of mine, Cameron Henrion, whose family I mentioned we had visited in Detroit on that twenty-state journey. While we had been working on developing grassroots community empowerment blueprints, he had been working on developing alternative economic systems that were also focused on empowering people outside of the typical systems of debt and bondage. Seven years before, God had given me the name of a company or something of the sort, KBR, which was part of an Aramaic word that means, "place of abundance." I didn't know specifically what it would be for at the time, but there were three things I believed to be involved whenever something was to come about with that name; those were gold, land and business.

So, it worked out well years later when Cameron had developed this alternative, economic system that would be a community-based and gold-backed business. It just so happened that the flow of Cameron's system matched the empowerment concepts of our community blueprints perfectly. It was a natural match in that regard, and he then adopted the name KBR as the name of the system he had created.

What is amazing is that how during this season Destiny was literally pregnant with and about to birth our eighth child, Abundance, Cameron, his team and I started working towards implementing a pilot version of the KBR system in Ethiopia and some other communities we were involved with to a different degree, essentially aiming to lay the groundwork to create or empower places of abundance.

Meanwhile, we found ourselves back based in Cody, WY, preparing for Abundance to come in February. This season was about preparing, and we weren't supposed to go or travel until after she had come. We believe she marked a new season beginning. After the check-ups and ultrasounds that Destiny had in Jerusalem, she continued to research and prepare as best she knew. We prayed about whether we should seek that avenue, not wanting to automatically assume we would have another natural, unassisted, at-home birth again, even though that's what Destiny wanted most.

Back at the beginning of the pregnancy, when Destiny had a few scares, I was asking the Lord where His grace was for this pregnancy, birth and delivery, and how He wanted us to go about it. The primary thing that rang loudly was I sensed from the Lord that this time wasn't about an angel of supernatural birth or anything of that sort, but that this pregnancy — and the delivery — would, for me at least, be about using my authority in Christ through prayer — like when we thought there might have been a miscarriage at the beginning of this pregnancy. Honestly, that wasn't what I wanted to sense from the Lord on the subject as if it was my choice. But I realized naturally that if I was going to have to use my authority during the process, then that likely meant that there were going to be some tough moments or obstacles that we were going to face. Personally, I preferred the last at-home, unassisted birth that went so supernaturally smoothly! And the thought of us having no professional care while also having potential complications was a worrisome thought. However, I knew I could trust the Lord. I just needed to keep listening and be willing to go seek other care if He directed us to.

That's often the hardest part about living the way we do, those moments of in-between tension where all you want to do is the "right" thing, and yet you don't always have certainty of what the right thing is. Instead, it's trusting God in those unknown moments, knowing that He is not playing games with us with His voice, and we just need to follow the Holy Spirit's convictions and directives. It can feel much easier to go all-in-one way, saying, "we're just going to do this by faith again!" Or to get nervous, panic and preempt the process by bringing in unnecessary interventions that can make things even harder. We realized during this labor and delivery that's what happened with

William's birth before his emergency C-section. Some of man's ways (our own included) caused interventions that might not have been necessary. Holy Spirit reminded us of these moments, as well as specific moments with Aliyah's birth that were great learning experiences.

Destiny remained sure that she wanted to go the unassisted, at-home route, and as long as I/we didn't hear the Lord say something else, we would stick with that plan. It got hard though. In the weeks leading up to Abundance's birth, there was some unusual pre-labor that was start and stop in a very different way than she had before with all her other pregnancies. Enough started a couple of times that we wondered if there were complications or if we needed to go see someone. But the Lord just kept preaching patience to our hearts. Specifically, He gave us the promise in James those last few weeks that reminds us:

"But let patience have its perfect work, that you may be perfect and complete, lacking nothing." (James 1:4)

I began to camp on that promise strongly. In any moment of question, worry or doubt, I could go back to that word from Him as our rock. Unless or until He said otherwise, patience was our path. And when we have a word like that from the Lord, it helps us know how to wield the sword of His word, essentially, how to use our authority. I began to declare that word over Destiny and Abundance many times a day as we waited, sometimes concerned with where the process was or wasn't. I claimed and spoke that the result of our patience of waiting on the Lord would result in the baby, Destiny, and labor and delivery all to be "perfect and complete, lacking nothing," according to this path of patience with Him.

Finally, the day before our actual due date, after two-plus weeks of start and stop labor, it felt like it was the day Abundance was going to be born. I remember being out on a walk that morning and finding myself declaring another verse from Micah 2:13 about the Lord as our breaker, going before us at our head. I didn't just ask for it that day but declared that He was going before us, breakthrough was starting, and Abundance was going to be born that day. This whole last month, the kids had been gathering around Destiny, praying and contending over her and the baby. Like most of these adventures in our lives, it had truly been a family affair. And many, many others were praying too!

That afternoon, Des was playing a card game with the kids when suddenly, those contractions started to ramp up fast and furious. They weren't much different from all the start and stop times, but we believed this was the time. Ayni and Dave came and picked up the kids so Destiny could focus, and that's when she got her game face on.

After a couple of hours, labor was progressing well, except Destiny was now in a ton of pain. For someone who has birthed many children, she knows the different types of pain well. She said this was different, though, and I had never seen her battle and scream in this much pain. It seemed like Abundance was stuck, like the way Will had been before his emergency C-section. I stayed right behind her, helping hold her hips, and we just prayed and declared promise after promise from the Lord. It got so intense that I knew we needed another level of the Lord's power, so I began to pray out loud in the Holy Spirit. I started off softly, but quickly felt something start to rise within, saying to use that authority. My prayer language jumped a few notches to a focus and dialect that I had never heard come out of me before. But as I did, I started seeing this vision of heaven just pouring out and flowing down into Destiny and her womb. And every time, she would get quieter and more peaceful during those moments. Later, Des told me that whenever I prayed in that specific dialect in the Spirit, she felt as if heaven was just flowing down into her and bringing so much peace. It was wild hearing her describe the exact vision I saw as I prayed during those moments. The more we handled it that way, the more she progressed, until she was ready to go and try to push in the bathtub. The battle continued, and so we kept trying to handle it through the authority of prayer and the word as much as possible. And then suddenly, everything shifted, and Abundance was on her way out and Destiny was co-laboring with the Lord to bring her fully to life.

I caught her in that moment, looking to make sure she was okay. She cried to open up and clear her lungs and I couldn't believe she was already trying to open her eyes. I scanned back and forth and saw that God's promise from James was fulfilled, she was perfect and complete, lacking nothing. Despite the battle, God brought us through the process in His own unique way and all she had was a little mark on her forehead where you could tell she had been stuck, and likely what was causing Destiny so much pain.

Destiny sighed with obvious, deep relief, but even more with those tears of absolute thankfulness and joy! God had done it again. She had done it again. And our Abundance was here! Just like her name, Adi, she was the greatest gift we could receive. Her middle name is Tzion, a Hebrew name for Zion since that's where her precious life began. And now, we were ready to throw our nets on the "other side of the boat" as John 21 talks about, and like our forty days of abundance, see a new kind of shift to steward forward with the Lord.

But like those 40 days of abundance that we learned years ago back in Colorado, it wasn't, and isn't, about the resources we do or do not have. It's about how we live by faith with what we have in our hands. It can be little, or it can be much. It can be seemingly not enough, or it can be an abundance. No matter which season we are in, both must be stewarded with forward-moving faith, and only His voice could continue to lead us there.

In Matthew 25 and Luke 19, we read the parables Jesus taught about the Talents and the Minas. Both are incredible teachings in many facets. But one part sticks out to me that is the same in both. The Parable of the Talents in Matthew 25 wraps up in verse 29 with this: *"For to everyone who has, more will be given, and he will have an abundance..."*

And the Parable of the Minas is very similar. Luke 19:26 says, *"For I say to you, that to everyone who has will be given..."*

Jesus teaches us at the end of both these parables this truth, that *"he who has,"* more will be given, and he *"will have an abundance."* What this reminds us is that if we are waiting for God's promise of abundance, or for a wealth transfer or Joseph like season, it is important that we learn, like Paul, to live like "one who has." When we become a people who already have, we will naturally attract the abundance to us so that it can move and multiply through us.

This is not a fake it untilyou make it kind of thing. This is a genuinely believe and recognize you are full on the inside before you receive on the outside. If we will help usher in a season of abundance in the Body of Christ to build His kingdom during this very special time ahead, we will first learn to live like "one who has." Our need doesn't attract abundance, rather, our internal fullness does. Often, if you see someone in need you are more naturally prone to give to the extent to just meet their need. But when you see someone walking in something powerful or full of life, you want to give more abundantly to add to it and even help it multiply. It's a natural principle Jesus was reminding us of.

So, as you anticipate the amazing promises God is birthing that we all love to talk about, remember that, like for my wife, you are first full of Abundance growing in you before you or the world reap the blessings of abundance in your hands.

If you are waiting for abundance, prepare like "one who has."

chapter 23

again

Just recently, we were on another one of our family's faith adventures on the road. We traveled over five thousand miles across a number of states, with two primary stops. But as many of the trips mentioned before — as well as some we didn't get to share — this recent trip once again began with us barely having the funding to even get started. First, a couple of hundred dollars came in that helped us prepare for the trip as we planned to get on our way by faith, and it helped fill up our gas tank to make it to our first overnight stop. But our first planned destination would still be a couple more days' drive away. We planned to be in east Texas for a week but still didn't have the money to book our Air BnB there yet; we needed $300 just to put down a deposit to reserve it and start payments on such. We felt strongly we were still supposed to go. Late that night about 9:30 pm, I remember talking to the Lord, saying, "We could really use a little boost here, Lord," clearly starting to feel the realities of the kind of trip we were once again starting. About thirty minutes later, there was a knock on our front window. It was our neighbor, Adrian. *"I felt from the Lord you guys needed this,"* he said. It was $300 exactly. At ten o'clock at night. And the rest of the trip for three and a half weeks continued along those same lines, day by day watching God show up and help us take the next step, or pay the next bill.

We share this because you get to a point sometimes where you want to say, "Lord, You know we trust You, but do we really have to go through it this way again? Haven't we learned this yet?" And perhaps we have, but that doesn't take away the value from the process.

It makes me think of a scene from the movie, Miracle, the Disney movie about the 1980 USA men's hockey team whose victory over Russia was dubbed, "The miracle on ice." There is one scene in the movie where the team is in Sweden, going through an exhibition match to get ready for the Olympic games. They played terrible, just awful, uninspiring hockey. The coach was trying to draw out something more.

So, after their lackluster effort, he kept the players on the ice for some postgame conditioning. The players skate the ice, already exhausted, barely able to believe more is being required of them.

Coach Herb Brooks announces to the players, and the assistant blowing the whistle, *"Again!"* And the players skate again.

"Again!" They finish yet another round of skating.

"Again!" Brooks yells methodically, unmoved by the opinions forming around him.

"Again!"

This time he just looks and nods, *"Send them again."*

This happens so many times after the game mind you, that the players are incredulous, the arena staff are turning off the lights because they want to go home, and even the coaching staff starts to turn on Brooks.

"Again." Brooks declares in an unemotional reply.

The players are beyond exhausted now, coughing, throwing up, on their knees.

One player, barely able to catch his breath, breaks the pattern.

"Mike Eruzione," he cries out, stating his name out loud the way they did in their original team introductions.

Fighting to get words beyond his shortness of breath, he cries out again, declaring where he is from. That, too, was typical of their introductions.

But then Eruzione started to try to offer something different, something more.

Coach Brooks stopped, and replied loudly to Eruzione, *"Who do you play for?"*

The player, still gasping for air, finally got out the words, *"I play for the United States of America."* His response differing from how the players had always replied, usually stating the college team they were associated with.

"That's all gentleman," Brooks said as he suddenly walked off the ice.

The players and coaches all understood it now. Coach Brooks wasn't making them go again and again without a deeper reason. He was trying to extract something more from them. He was looking for an uncommon response to build an uncommon team of men.

He kept telling them to go again because he knew there was more in front of them, more inside them. "Again" was part of the way forward.

Here is a quote I've heard and read from multiple places and people, but this one says it well, and clearly: ***The word "testimony" comes from the Hebrew word 'eduth.' This word literally means 'do it again with the same power and authority.' So, when we speak out or even read a testimony, we're literally saying, 'Do it again, God.'"*** (from Tithe.ly, The Power of Your Story)

I share this because our testimonies aren't supposed to just stop after one miracle. God wants to "do it again." We should too. There is more He is leading us towards, more ground to take, more lives for His kingdom. He wants to do it again, even if He doesn't always do it the same way.

Have you ever had one of those conversations with a friend or one of your kids where you are posed with the question: "If you could pick any superpower, what would it be?" Most people tend to land on answers such as going back in time, flying, invisibility, etc. Now, imagine that you were granted one of these giftings and you learned how to fly.

You wouldn't just use this superpower once, would you? I highly doubt any of us would take our first flight, arms spread like an eagle, thrusting our fists forward in the air like superman, only to decide, "alright, I'm good. No more flying for me."

That would be outrageous. Right?

I mean, who would learn a superpower only to give it up without putting it to good use for a lifetime of defying the odds, adventure, helping others and unadulterated joy?

Well, someone who had a rough first flight, that's who. Same with someone who misused their power of invisibility. Or who messed up the future by traveling back in time. The hypothetical superpower conversation is only fun when talking about the glorious parts that accompany it. Rarely do we think about, let alone understand, the cost it might come with.

That cost is somewhere between the realities that come with the "flying," and the process of navigating those realities. It's easier to talk about heroic hypotheticals than it is to put something unknown and uncommon to actual, consistent use.

Many of us have probably read or heard the story of when Jesus was on the water and called Peter out of the boat. Like many of the miracles the disciples were privy to, I imagine we stand in awe of these supernatural occurrences we read about. But, judging by the text, I don't think it likely felt all that miraculous.

I mean, it sounds like it started to. Peter heard Jesus' call, he stepped out of the boat with his heart probably clamped down somewhere between his faith and his intellect, his fear and his trust, his worry and his hope or desire for something more. And that's when that first "flight" all started to go seemingly awry. Peter started to sink.

"And Peter answered Him and said, 'Lord, if it is You, command me to come to You on the water.' So He said, 'Come.' And when Peter had come down out of the boat, he walked on the water to go to Jesus.

But when he saw that the wind was boisterous, he was afraid; and beginning to sink he cried out, saying, 'Lord, save me!'

And immediately Jesus stretched out His hand and caught him, and said to him, 'O you of little faith, why did you doubt?'"

(Matthew 14: 28-31)

So, going back to our whole superpower conversation. Who would want to walk on water if it meant sinking in the middle of the sea? Jesus was trying to teach Peter to walk by something that no human had ever operated by, something that most of us can only dream about — but Peter might have had a different feeling about it when he continued to plummet into the stormy waters.

I think my question starts there. What would Peter have done if Jesus asked Peter to do it again?

Walking on water shouldn't be just to say you've done it, or only to share the story with others. Walking on water, or any of the superpowers, if you will, teaches you to navigate the world in a new way. And therefore, hopefully, to accomplish things in the kingdom that you and possibly others couldn't or even wouldn't have before. Walking on water is learned to be another tool in your toolbelt, another way to go forward where others don't know how. It helps us access what most are not accessing. Walking by faith is something we learn so that we can do it again because it's usually the only way to go into new seasons, new territory, and how to go places with Jesus that we otherwise would only read about. "Again" isn't a punishment, or a re-test, it's an invitation to walk in the "more" that God has made available to us.

river life vs. pond culture:

"He who believes in Me, as the Scripture has said, out of his heart will flow rivers of living water.' But this He spoke concerning the Spirit..." (John 7:38-39)

Walking on water leads us to the counter-cultural path Jesus lived out so perfectly. It's an integral facet of the life that honors the Holy Spirit and gives Him room to lead and flow out of our lives, transforming our life and path rather than fitting Him into our ways or comfort zones. It's something we continue to learn to live and surrender to. It doesn't just lead us to Jesus, the way Peter was walking to Him, but it can teach us to live a different path entirely.

WALKING ON WATER

We are told that there is a River inside us that flows with living water! The very fact that it flows highlights its movement and is what sustains its living nature. When you take water and make it stagnant, such as with a pond, though it is still technically water that can be shared with a thirsty world, it is also water that begins to grow fungus and disease from standing still too long. Wouldn't the fungus and disease that grows on standing water be contrary to the pure, living nature of the water we are promised is within us? Yet, it is so easy to take the rivers of the Holy Spirit from within us and form Him into controllable ponds contained by our well-meaning edges that we construct because of fear, man, and the influences of culture around us. When we honor the place of oneness with the Holy Spirit and His leadership in our lives, we empower Him to flow out of us like the river He came to be; always moving, always leading, us in Him and Him in us, and we become an ever-flowing river of life that brings healing and life to the world — wherever we go.

Ponds are an easy, cultural justification to fall into. It's still the Spirit's living water that we are offering, after all. We are still giving it to a thirsty world. But with such standing water, what other man-made fungus and disease are we contaminating His living water with? Are we changing the way God's true nature should be revealed? Is our struggle to surrender to the Holy Spirit's lead adding our fungus and disease to what the world would be tasting of Him? Does our fear of losing control remove the purity of water that could actually heal and give life to the world?

The world around us has had plenty of fungus and bad bacteria growing, and it is dying for a taste of the pure, living water Jesus came to bring. But that's impossible if we don't live something different, something contrary to cultural expectations, and choose to live a life that is always moving forward and giving the world a fresh taste of the Living God. The water they were created to long for becomes available when we make His river more freely available through how we lead and live. I do believe God is a God of order. However, that does not necessarily mean that we provide the order. That is one of the ways we honor the Spirit, by trusting in His secure control rather than our control, allowing ourselves to be shaken from those familiar, counterfeit securities of the world so that the whole world might know He who has already made them secure. The world must not taste of any more ponds constructed in the Spirit's honor but of the pure life-giving river waiting to flow freely out of us.

The River led life is not easy. It's easy to say that we believe in it, but it is a whole other matter to trust Him in this oneness and what can look like an unpredictable, winding river. That is where honor comes in. We honor His unseen over our seen. We honor His eyes over our eyes. We honor His control over our fears and wounds. We honor His security over our insecurities. We honor His shaken, winding movement over our own sure-footed, unshaken stance. The pond may look more secure from the outside, but its threat of disease growing over time while stagnant is guaranteed and much more dangerous. The River looks to move outside of our control, and unpredictably so. But He is sure to always have His own bounds, always guide us over the right terrain, through the right seasons at the right pace, and He is sure to flow with living water that brings life wherever it goes.

When Destiny and I got married, we decided to choose an uncommon song for her to walk down the aisle to. We wanted a song that represented our new life together, how God was joining us together, and how He wanted us to live forward in oneness with one another, and Him. We began to ask God to show us what that song might be. We wanted to know the life He was launching us into together with Him. That is when we found our song. "Find Me In the River," by Delirious. For us, the Lord highlighted it as an obvious choice because one thing was clear for this new life together, we were about to start; we always wanted — and needed — to be found by God and by one another **in the River.**

Sadly, we don't always want leaders who are led by passion, or whose radical pursuit of the Lord challenges daily routines and worldly expectations. It requires that we live in the tension of the kingdom rather than by the black and white principles that we are taught by the world. It requires that we allow Truth to literally come alive beyond our current understanding of it in a whole new way. We often want leaders and lives that are tested, tried, proven and made into programs that will fulfill our needs and expectations, A+B=C. We don't always want the unpredictability that comes from keeping our eyes on the Spirit's lead, always joining Him where He is moving. Such can mean a change from the norm. But isn't that how Jesus surprised His disciples each day? Surprises were almost a guarantee when being led by One who always joined the Father where He was moving, and it's a vital part of seeing the whole of the Father's nature revealed to the world. We must let Him surprise us and trust Him with such. Remember, *He is a good God!*

With our eyes fixed on Him, and that being our first measure, our path might wind and weave. It might even start in one direction and then, like many rivers, double back in the other direction. The onlooking world may even see your river double back and say, "See, you were wrong and had to turn around." But that's not how God works. Sometimes He takes our life, like a river, in one direction just to pick up one seed or nutrient before He changes our direction because He wants us to carry that special seed to the dry and barren place that He's going to lead us through next. God is much more about faith and obedience in the process than the appearance of the result that man usually lives by. It shouldn't matter what worldly perception says our path looks like as much as Who we are looking at to be our path. Our path can look shaken when our eyes and focus are not actually shaken at all. Because our path is just adjusting to His, and God rarely works in our kind of linear ways.

When you follow a paved path, it is something that has been walked before and has clear boundaries. But when you follow a person, their path is your path, regardless of how it might look. How can we truly lead while following Jesus if we require such a pre-existing man-made structure and control already in place? There is control, but it comes through trusting Him.

This is the way of the river. It is living, moving, and seemingly unpredictable and unexplainable from the outside. The only predictability comes from knowing the nature and word of God. The nature of God is in the river. It's the most powerful place to live or lead from, but the toughest place to stay. This is the very reason we must be so shaken by our connection with God, that we might be unmoved by worldly perception and the fear of man. Those two things must no longer compel us to climb out of the river and prop up external appearance, putting our eyes back on the people. Remaining in the river requires us to trust the people's opinions and perceptions into God's hands and keep moving forward with Him. I always want to be found in the river, no matter what others may think it looks like.

Still, Destiny and I pray for us and our family to always be found in the river. That will probably look different for each person. It is marked by a counter-cultural, forward-moving path with the Lord without having to prove oneself nor protect what is comfortable. When we allow the ways of the river to challenge our ways of thinking, we'll see the kingdom of God start to come and offer a fresh contrast to the ways of the world, showing something new and alive while giving them living water straight from the Source.

And if I, or we, want to stay in the river, to live the counter-cultural life, ways and the fruit of Jesus, we must learn to walk on water. We must learn to live by grace, through faith. Like Peter, we have far too often felt the waves and storms taunting us. And that's when we try to put our eyes back on Jesus. That is when we listen for His voice, His call to step forward out of the boat, out of the box. That is when we obey regardless of whether we understand or not, surrendering ourselves to His ways and understanding above our own. And that is when He shows up. Jesus meets us, pours grace on us, strengthens our weaknesses, provides for us and so much more. He helps us catch our breath. Helps us rejoice in what He did and who He is!

And then, He calls us out on the water again, because the river isn't a moment just to cross; it's a life and a path to be lived so that we, and the world around us, will hopefully never be the same.

Joey and his wife, Destiny, have been married for 23 years. They have eight children and two grandchildren. As a family, they have both lived, and traveled, all around the world, empowering people to discover and live out who they were created to be. Joey has authored eleven books, and three children's books. As a family, they write and create to give life to a generation who will shine in the world.

LeTourneau
Creative

To see other books and projects by the author, please visit:
LeTourneau Creative

LeTourneaucreative.com

Heaven's Heart for Earth

Seraph Creative is a collective of artists, writers, theologians & illustrators who desire to see the body of Christ grow into full maturity, walking in their inheritance as Sons of God on the Earth.

Sign up to our newsletter to know about future exciting releases.

Visit our website : www.seraphcreative.org

www.ingramcontent.com/pod-product-compliance
Lightning Source LLC
Chambersburg PA
CBHW051522120626
46551CB00012B/1044